MULE DEER

MULE DEER

*How to Bring Home North America's
Big Deer of the West*

Norm Nelson

Photos by the author unless otherwise credited

Stackpole Books

Published by
STACKPOLE BOOKS
Cameron and Kelker Streets
P.O. Box 1831
Harrisburg, PA 17105

10   9   8   7   6   5   4   3   2   1

Printed in the United States of America

Library of Congress Cataloging-in-Publication Data

Nelson, Norm.
    Mule deer.

    Bibliography: p.
    Includes index.
    1. Mule deer hunting.   I. Title.
SK301.N35   1986   799.2'77357   86-23063
ISBN 0-8117-0984-1

Dedicated to
Jackie, Sandy, and Sally

Not surprisingly, great wives
produce great daughters

*   *   *

"For the hunter is the joy of the horse well ridden and the rifle well held; for him the long days of toil and hardship, resolutely endured and crowned at the end with triumph. In after-years there shall come forever to his mind the memory of endless prairies shimmering in the bright sun; of vast, snow-clad wastes . . . of the breath of the evergreen forest in summer; of the crooning of ice-armored pines at the touch of winds of winter; of cataracts roaring between hoary mountain masses; of all the innumerable sights and sounds of the wilderness; of its immensity and mystery; and of the silences that brood in its depths." — *Theodore Roosevelt*

Contents

16 After Your Game Is on the Ground   180

*Dead or Alive • Field Dressing • Does Rinsing Cause Spoilage? • Get a Horse
• Best Ways to Drag Game • Quartering and Boning • Bird and Bug Defenses
• Filchers in Fur Coats • Skinning and Cooling • Up or Down? • Play It Cool
• From Venison to Eatin' Meat • Avoid Overcooking • Caping a Trophy •
Meat Handling Hardware*

17 Mule Deer Hunting—Here Today, Gone Tomorrow?   189

*Are Muley Hunters an Endangered Species? • Different Kinds of Trophies •
The Rebirth of Market Hunting • "Quality of the Hunt" • Can We Overshoot the
Big Buck Resource? • Genetic Boomerangs • Should We Restrict Trophy Hunt-
ing? • The Nonresident Rip-off • Whose Land? • Normans vs. Saxons •
Changes in Hunting • Farewell to Free and Easy • The Energy Boom, Past,
Present and Future • Today's Poaching Menace • The Slob Problem • How
We're Loving the West to Death • Winter Habitat Wipeout • Guess Where the
Antihunters are Now, and Why • Who Pays for Wildlife Conservation? • Reve-
nue Realities • How to Defend Your Hunting Rights • Let's Get Politics Back into
Conservation • A Heritage for the Grandchildren*

Foreword

Deer hunters pass through three stages of development. The first stage comes when you have a few years of experience and have downed a few deer. At that point, you have all the answers. The next stage comes when you have put perhaps fifteen seasons behind you and have seen enough strange things to wonder if you have *any* answers at all. The final stage occurs at twenty-five-plus years. Then even the strange stuff sorts itself out into a pattern and you can say with some conviction that you do know what you're talking about.

Norm Nelson definitely falls into the third category. He started mule deer hunting in 1952, which gives him more than three decades of matching wits with *Odocoileus hemionus* in different parts of the West. I have a fair amount of experience myself but when I find someone with this kind of credential, I listen.

In 1952, mule deer country was a lot different than it is now, as Norm reports in this book. The deer herds had profited from World War II and the resulting drop in hunter pressure. The Korean War was in progress as well, and this too tended to make the job of being a mule deer easier. The result was large herds of big deer that were not particularly wary, wide open land, and ranchers who tended to look at you queerly if you asked permission to hunt their land. Why, they said, should that be necessary?

Well, today out there on the lone prairie where the coyote howls and the wind blows free, there ain't much else that's free any more. Licenses are sold on the quota or lottery system and usually are gone in short order. Where once hunters appeared in squad and platoon strength, they now operate in reinforced brigades and divisions. There are still good numbers of mule deer (although this can change very quickly with a couple of hard winters back to back). And there are still some very big deer.

But there are no more big dumb deer. The forty-inch-rack buck that once would stand and look at you as you umlimbered to shoot him is now as clever and paranoid as his white-tailed cousin, which is very clever and very paranoid indeed.

But the most profound change has been in the people who control the private lands — the ranchers and farmers. Almost all of these folks can, tell you hair-raising stories of hunter vandalism. And I can tell you that if you want to avoid serious trouble, you had best ask their permission to hunt. Even more important is the growing awareness on their part that game animals are a cash crop — and in many cases, an important cash crop.

I have hunted in northeastern Wyoming a number of years now. The land there is almost entirely private. The ranchers who own it will be pleased to let you on, put you up, and guide you — for a fee. That can range anywhere from a few hundred dollars for a few days to two thousand for five days. (This last is a very limited hunt for major trophy bucks.) What was once a casual and easily accessible sport has now become one of limited supply and great demand. A beginning hunter (or even an intermediate hunter) no longer has the luxury of setting out with a heart full of hope and a brain full of ignorance, trusting that it will all work out okay. Nine times out of ten, he will encounter nothing but frustration and disappointment. In short, nothing can take the place of experience. But this book will help.

A word about Norm Nelson. He comes from a hunting family and started on whitetails in Minnesota at age twelve in 1940. Good taste forbids my saying how many deer he has taken, but I know it's a bunch. I have known Norm as an outdoor writer for about fifteen years. Take my word that Norm is, for lack of a better word, a character. In addition to a passion for the outdoors, he is keenly interested in politics and history; and this crops up at the oddest times. Several times on the occasions I've hunted mule deer with him, he has slammed on the pickup's brakes for nothing I could see and turned to me with a face full of ancestral Viking wrath. "Dave!" he would bellow, "How on earth could Roosevelt sell us out at Yalta like that?" Then he would calmly drive on as if nothing had happened.

He is also given to rhapsodizing about such diverse things as Labrador Retrievers and obsolete cameras and writes long single-spaced letters filled with politics, hunting anecdotes, shooting lore, and general calumny. I burn them after reading, since even one of these virulent epistles would get him sued by twenty-five special interest groups if it fell into the wrong hands.

Oh, yes. On each of two hunts with Norm, he has steered me into mule deer bucks good enough to hang on my wall. If I were you, I would listen to the guy.

Dave Petzal, Executive Editor
Field & Stream
1987

Introduction

When Chet Fish of Stackpole Books first approached me to do a book on hunting mule deer, we kicked the idea around a bit. I told him that I was not interested in doing what the outdoor media call the "me and Joe" approach, involving a long personal litany of mule deer taken in the past.

My belief is that the readers are much more interested in what *they* can accomplish as hunters rather than what an author has accomplished. So this is basically a how-to book for people interested in hunting mule deer more effectively and more enjoyably.

When I cite personal hunting episodes by way of explaining certain points in mule deer hunting, I sometimes use examples of "ones that got away." When the quarry instead of the hunter wins, the hunter should learn something from the experience.

Anyone who hunts the big, intelligent, fast-learning muley bucks will often lose the contest with an individual deer. That's what makes mule deer hunting a highly challenging outdoor adventure. The hunter who sallies forth convinced that big mule deer are easy game is often licked before he starts. And frequently the weather and terrain are also formidable antagonists.

A serious mule deer hunter will find it profitable to do other reading on the subject. Long out of print but available through larger libraries is Ernest Thompson Seton's classic *Lives of Game Animals*, of which Volume III covers mule deer and their relatives. Seton's decades-old material is incomplete and in some cases superseded by better knowledge, but he was a great nature writer and magnificent wildlife artist.

The Wildlife Management Institute in 1981 published *Mule & Black-tailed Deer of North America*, a potpourri of treatises by various wildlife experts. It suffers from the unfortunate obsession of professional wildlifers to use their own scientific jargon, making it heavy reading for the layman.

For the hunter, the most interesting chapter in *Mule & Black-tailed Deer of North America* is one on mule deer behavior, written by Valerius Geist, professor of environmental science at the University of Calgary in Alberta. He explains the reasons for some interesting things in the life and times of mule deer that many of us have long noted and wondered about without really understanding them. Dr. Geist is that all-too-rare combination of highly observant scientist *and* good communicator. May his tribe increase.

Much easier to read is Leonard Lee Rue's *The Deer of North America*, which of course is only in part about mule deer. A couple of recent books on mule deer hunting are Jim Zumbo's *Hunting America's Mule Deer* and Kirt Darner's *How to Find Giant Bucks*. Muleys are always included in the deer hunting annuals produced by such magazines as *Field & Stream, Guns & Ammo*, and *Outdoor Life*. Hunting the big western deer is also routinely covered in the monthly outdoor magazines. And worthwhile articles related to arms and ammo suitable for mule deer hunting appear in such gunpowder stalwarts as *Gun Digest* and *Gun Annual*.

Throughout my past 30-plus years in mule deer hunting and in doing this book, I've drawn on the help and thoughts of a number of people, some of them excellent hunters in their own right, all of them fine folks in the bargain: Joy, Dean, Kurt, and the late Ernest Hall; Randy and Gail Buckley; Pat and Jim McFall (that's a pair to draw to); Craig Boddington of Petersen's *Hunting* magazine; Ken Warner of *Gun Digest*; and the inimitable Dave Petzal of *Field & Stream*. Dave is one of those unflappable people in any crisis, be it making a one-shot kill on a deer at 300 yards or eating my camp cookery. Finally I must cite a chap named Peter Nelson who has been my hunting buddy for at least thirty years and my son for thirty-six years, patiently putting up with me in both roles.

If you enjoy hunting mule deer, I have a hunch you'll enjoy this book.

Norm Nelson
Federal Way, Washington
1987

1

Meet the Mule Deer

.

The big buck made a news photo only because it was hit by a car and created a traffic jam on a major beltline arterial in Minneapolis. The now-defunct Minneapolis Star predictably missed the real grabber. The buck was a mule deer with the unmistakable forked antlers and black skullcap.

Why was that news? Because this big stranger was close to four hundred miles from what's supposed to be the eastern limit of Rocky Mountain mule deer range. What led him from the short-grass prairies across the wide Missouri into a 1.5-million-people metro area that far east is still a puzzler twenty-five years later.

That's mule deer for you. About the time you think you've got them figured out, they surprise you again. Or maybe the Ulyssean wanderings of the big beltline buck shouldn't be startling. Mule deer of various subspecies have managed to homestead from central Mexico's octillo and cactus up to the Canadian subarctic's Land of Little Sticks. At their western range limits, muleys on a clear day can see salt water from the Cascades' crest. We marvel at the adaptability of white-tailed deer. Yet mule deer, living in the shriveling heat of the Sonoran desert or taking 150 degrees below zero wind chill factor in stride in the Yukon, deserve some kind of Harsh Environments Campaign Ribbon too.

This great animal's names make many of us wince. The scientific label, *Odocoileus hemionus*, is partly erroneous Greek, roughly meaning hollow-toothed and mulelike, both misleading labels. The large ears are responsible for the mule or ass comparison and this carries over into the term *burro deer* for the smallest subspecies, found in the Southwest and Mexico. It leads to confusion among nonhunters, who wonder if this means a deer that looks like a mule, or vice versa. Learning that I hunted them, a horse-worshipping lady once snapped, "MULE deer? Aren't they legally protected like wild horses and burros?" She was serious.

The naturalist-artist Ernest Thompson Seton thought they should be called hill deer. Although mule deer are found in plains areas, uplands are their more common home. More recently, a now-deceased guns-and-hunting writer, who habitually confused himself with Moses toting the Commandments, often thundered against the diminutive of "muley." Those of us with more important concerns in life find "muley" a useful speaking, writing, and reading relief from constant repetition of "mule deer." (For similar reasons, sometimes I unabashedly use "whitetail" for cousin *Odocoileus virginianus* instead of "white-tailed deer," which after the twentieth time begins to sound like a medieval Gregorian chant.)

Of mule deer subspecies, more later in this chapter. What about them as game animals? Are they as challenging to hunt as the more widely chronicled whitetail? Or is an opinionated friend of mine right when he calls mule deer hunting not a big-game adventure but more like king-size varmint shooting? What are the muley's strengths and weaknesses as fair-chase quarry?

The life history of mule deer as it is known today from scientific study is too long for a hunting book as such. But for the particular interest of a hunter audience, here are some major features of the mule deer as we know and love it:

1. Compared to whitetails, mule deer are much more herd animals, although mature bucks at times live apart from does and younger deer. Herds of game are always easier to locate than single animals. However, with multiplied eyes, ears, and noses on guard for danger, stalking herds can be difficult.

2. Mule deer are much calmer, less jittery animals than the habitually nervous whitetails. This even shows up in captive deer where muleys become tame faster and more thoroughly than do whitetails.

3. The common belief that a muley is less intelligent than a whitetail is a misunderstanding of muley defense tactics. A lot of mule deer range offers little concealment. With no place to hide, putting safe distance between oneself and danger is the only game in town. Yet after an initial getaway spurt, the mule deer often stops to look back. Stupidity? No—tactical necessity. Before making its next survival play, the deer must know where the predator is, whether it's still pursuing, how closely, and for that matter, how many predators are there. For eons, this look-back analysis helped muleys as a species to survive enemies who (bow-hunting Indians included) were a threat only at fairly close range.

Then came a new, rifle-packing predator dangerous at ten times the distance of the long-familiar venison eaters. Some of us believe that modern mule deer are fast learning fresh survival tactics to cope with this different menace. Mammals are an evolutionary success because they learn well. Like the whitetail, the mule deer has a relatively large brain,

Not just a splendid trophy, the mule deer in various subspecies is a highly adaptable, challenging big-game species from the deserts of Mexico almost to the Arctic Circle. This big buck is a Rocky Mountain mule deer, the biggest, most widely distributed of the muley family. — *Wyoming Game Department Photo*

one hallmark of animal learning ability. Hunters, guides, and ranchers increasingly note that many big muley bucks no longer pause for that famous last look back at a pursuer, traditionally an easier shot than a muley on the bound. And they've become much more nocturnal, at least in hunting season.

My belief is that under increased hunting pressure, muleys learn to put more reliance on timber cover, just as elk had to do. To survive the onslaught of gun-packing pioneers, American elk rapidly learned to abandon their ancestral plains for better security in heavily forested mountains. We may underestimate how quickly hard-hunted game can adapt. Three decades ago, I never saw spooked pronghorn antelope run up into steep hills. Now it's a common pronghorn escape tactic.

Although commonly associated with the West's open rangelands and deserts, muleys adapt very well to forest country. Author photographed this doe in big timber west of Cody, Wyoming.

4. In keeping with their open environment, mule deer have better vision than do whitetails. Researchers say muleys can spot other deer at six hundred yards. From experience, I'm convinced they can both see and recognize tall bipedal humans even farther *if* the human is moving. All deer do poorly at recognizing stationary humans even very close. But legally required safety colors may be another story. The bad news that science now tells us is that such animals are not color blind and that blaze orange may catch their eyes as readily as it does ours. Obviously that puts new demands on a hunter's craftiness.

The muley's ears and nose are excellent. On a calm day, I got the attention of a herd of feeding mule deer at a Rangematic-measured nine hundred yards from my Wyoming tent camp by turning up a portable radio not much higher than normal human voice level. In atmospheric conditions not ideal for scenting, I've had muleys wind me beyond four hundred yards (see Chapter 12).

5. A muley shows alarm by stiff posture, flaring its white rump, and holding the tail horizontally. Young bucks and does hold heads high then, but older bucks often assume a head-low stance. Rarely, an upset muley nostril-snorts. Retreat gait ranges from a purposeful trot to the fully alarmed series of high springing bounds, as if the legs were pogo sticks. Wildlife experts call this *stotting*. This doesn't cover ground as fast as a low-bounding whitetail, but the high bounds create difficulties for four-legged predators and marksmen (see Chapter 6).

6. To all deer, the mountain lion is terror personified, and far more frightening than mere human disturbance. Researchers find that lion activity can cause muleys to quickly vacate a sizable area. During one season, the appearance of a big tom cougar (that I saw) was followed in the next twenty-four to thirty-six hours by desertion of a two-square-mile timbered basin by most of the resident deer. If you find much lion sign in your muley area, go elsewhere to hunt. Big-cat presence will kibosh your hunting.

A lion guide told me that over half the cougar-killed deer he's found were sizable bucks. Studies of mountain lion kills show about seventy-five percent are adult bucks. One researcher guessed this was due to big bucks and mountain lions coincidentally using higher elevations. I think he missed the key point. At any elevation, including that of lowland whitetails, cougars go for usually solitary bucks simply because such loners are easier to stalk than a herd with its many eyes, ears, and noses on guard.

Coyotes are always a menace to fawns and occasionally (in deep snow) to mature deer. But sometimes tables are turned. My hunting partner Pat McFall, a retired game warden and skilled wildlife observer, watched three full-sized coyotes attempt to surround a mature muley (sex unknown since it was midwinter, after bucks had shed antlers). Without warning, the deer suddenly rushed the closest coyote and savagely hammered it with its front hooves, which are wicked weapons. The other two coyotes fled at once, as did the battered one. On this job, the coyotes didn't even make expenses, let alone a profit.

7. Mule deer eat a tremendous variety of different foods — over seven hundred plants, grasses, and parts of trees have been documented so far. Their food preferences vary with time of year as well as geographic loca-

Remains of a mule-deer fawn that was apparently killed by coyotes. A mountain lion usually covers its kill with branches and leaves. Although coyotes are a major menace to mule-deer fawns, full-grown muleys have been known to counterattack coyotes, sometimes with dire results for the coyotes.

tion. As one dedicated researcher, Dr. Valerius Geist, points out, what mule deer eat depends more on their choice of habitat than on the food itself. Furthermore, mule deer, in routinely sampling so many different foods, make it hard even for trained observers to tell where and how they have been feeding. Mule deer probably do more grazing than whitetails as a rule, but again that depends on what given habitats have to offer.

8. Mule deer breeding is worth a hunter's understanding for obvious tactical benefits. The rutting season is similar to that of whitetails—mid-autumn in the north but as late as December or January farther south. Bucks do some antler rubbing on convenient brush, similar to that for which whitetails are noted. Yet muleys do not make the prominent earthen scrapes of whitetails.

Buck rivalries before the peak of the rut involve threatening displays of dominance, including snorting and hissing, by the superior buck to intimidate his lesser rival. Oddly, antler size or development is not a guideline to buck dominance. When the bucks are unevenly matched, they may do some minor sparring with antlers, similar to a pair of men arm wrestling. Not true combat, according to trained researchers like the observant Dr. Geist, sparring matches do not decide dominance rank. In fact, the two bucks may end by peacefully remaining together for a couple of days—the buddy system of bigger and smaller bucks often noted by hunters. (A hunting lesson here is that, when spotting a buck mule deer, look sharply for a possible bigger companion nearby).

Real winner-take-all battle involves bucks more evenly matched and almost always older animals. These fights usually happen at the peak of the rut. The mellow muley is commonly regarded as less belligerent than his more excitable whitetail cousin. Maybe so, but in a real test, big mule deer with their great strength and antler armament are formidable. Geist saw one buck so violently antler-yanked off balance that it was stood on its head. (Closely related Columbia blacktails are powerful fighters, too. One biologist saw a buck hurl his opponent over his head. Call that gladiator a Black Belt blacktail.)

Antlers foremost, muley bucks attack with very fast, low, close-range rushes. If antlers lock, one trick is to suddenly pull an opponent off balance, then force him sideways. Woe to the buck thus caught in the flank, because he risks severe goring. The hide of one five-year-old buck showed forty-seven cuts, presumably from rutting warfare. Fatalities seem to be rare, but both bucks are likely to die if their antlers lock permanently. The fight ends when the beaten buck disengages and runs, the victor jabbing him with antler thrusts punctuated by barking coughs.

The loser usually is driven away from the home range of the doe group—the cause of the whole ruckus.

9. To learn when a doe is in estrus for breeding requires sampling of her urine by the buck. Within the limitations described in Chapter 12, this may make him vulnerable to the hunter's use of doe scent as an attractant. Courting by a muley buck can be a furtively patient stalk in which he actually mimics a fawn to disarm the doe's reluctance about his close approach. (Deer normally do not crowd one another. Nor do they stare at each other except as a dominance-establishing threat). Less common is the rush courtship with the buck in fast pursuit of the doe over a limited area. Yet throughout these courtship complexities, the dominant buck must often fend off the lesser bucks who are trying to court the does he's patiently tending for their eventual estrus. Small wonder that bucks can lose up to twenty-five percent of their pre-rut weight.

10. Also important to the hunter is the doe-search roaming done by normally furtive mule deer bucks. Sometimes this includes "horning," in which a wandering buck clashes his antlers against objects. Although they listen to horning by other bucks, few muleys answer with horning of their own or try to seek out other bucks sounding off this way. When hunters successfully attract mule deer bucks by antler rattling, it's probably not a true horning response. Instead, it may draw unattached bucks who believe the clash of antlers signals a full-scale dominance fight over nearby does.

The rutting season finds mature bucks compelled to trade security for sex. Where hunting seasons run late enough to overlap the rut, that poses obvious opportunities for the mule deer hunter.

*　　*　　*

Of the estimated five-million-plus mule deer in North America, the biggest and most widespread subspecies is the Rocky Mountain type, *Odocoileus hemionus hemionus,* found from central Arizona and New Mexico to Canada's Yukon and Northwest Territories. This is the mule deer that Boone and Crockett Club headhunters dream about (see Chapter 17). The smaller California muley, *O. h. californicus,* is found in the Golden State's lower portions. The southern mule deer, *O. h. fuliginatus,* ranges from extreme southern California's coastal area down to Mexico's Baja Peninsula. At the lower end of the latter area is the peninsula mule deer, *O. h. peninsulae.* The best known of the southern subspecies is *O. h.*

crooki, the desert mule deer of southern California, Arizona, and New Mexico, which ranges down in Mexico.

From central California north into coastal British Columbia ranges the Columbia blacktail, *O. h. columbianus*, once considered a separate species, later changed to subspecies status. (An opposite view is that the blacktail is the basic stock from which all muleys evolved.) Blacktails and Rocky Mountain mule deer interbreed where their ranges meet along the Cascade Mountains. The true Columbia blacktail is a medium-sized deer with small antlers. The much bigger "blacktails," with far larger racks, in the Cascades interbreed with Rocky Mountain mulies and are not recognized by Boone and Crockett as true Columbia blacktails.

Both the habitat *and* habits of the forest-dwelling Columbia blacktail and the little north-to-Alaska Sitka blacktail, *O. h. sitkensis*, are so dissimilar from other mule deer that blacktail hunting is not topically appropriate for a book on hunting "mule deer." As game animals, blacktails have more in common with whitetails — except that blacktails are tougher to hunt, due to the density of their typical forest habitat.

*   *   *

Rocky Mountain muleys are bigger than whitetails — true or false?

The question as worded is haywire and should be tersely answered "invalid entry," as my computer diplomatically replies to a meaningless command. *Which* Rocky Mountain muleys? Those from dry, desolate habitat, or muleys living in Fat City on a mountain range's moister west side with lots of old fire burns or clearcuts full of browse? And *which* whitetails — malnourished runts from buck-law states or corn-fed farm-country deer? What's "bigger?" Select individuals? Or average sizes?

There is no systematic weight-recording system comparable to the well-known Boone and Crockett trophy-scoring criteria. All we have are a few big deer weight records, some spot-averages done in individual research programs, and a tremendous amount of guesswork — none of it on the light side, you may be sure.

In four- to five-year-old Rocky Mountain muley bucks, a live weight of about two hundred pounds seems par for the course. Equivalent-age whitetails from fat farmlands will beat that. Compared to stockier whitetails, Rocky Mountain muleys tend to be streamlined, long-legged deer that *look* like they should weigh more than they usually do.

The heaviest muleys on, we hope, honest record are in the four-hundred-pound range. Deer weight is a function of not just genetics, but diet too. Most mule deer live in hardscrabble, semi-arid environments. Not surprisingly, the bigger ones are found in better watered zones with higher quality browse. Still another factor in deer weights is that in colder northern latitudes, a species tends to be larger as a heat-conservation mechanism.

Almost all deer weight data is for field-dressed specimens. Different formulas are used for conversion to live-weight poundage. The simplest one calls for multiplying dressed weight by 1.2 to 1.3. Naturalist-photographer Leonard Lee Rue suggests a figure lower than 1.25 as the multiplier for big deer, because the innards are a smaller percentage of their bulk.

*   *   *

We all know the mule deer is a game animal. Is it a *great* game animal? If great means challenging to hunt, yes — assuming mature muley bucks, wise in their years, are the quarry. (Young muley bucks can do dumb things at times; but that's true of young anythings, as all parents, human or animal, will attest.)

Next question — is my answer based on anything except blind loyalty to the mule deer? In short, does the author know what he's talking about?

Unlike most outdoor writers, I have some decades of experience pursuing (with gun and camera) all three of what hunters (not zoologists) consider distinctly different deer game — muleys, whitetails, and blacktails. I freely grant that there are many hunters who know more than I about specific breeds — some specialists in whitetail hunting, others in mule deer hunting, a few (not many) in blacktail hunting. However, it's my good fortune to live in the one state — Washington — that has substantial huntable populations of all three deer (although I don't confine my hunting to that state). Oregon has some whitetails, but they're not major game there.

A strong case can be made that the high-strung whitetail — anywhere, East or West — is the spookiest and craftiest of American deer to hunt. The blacktail has a cover-sneaking lifestyle much more like the whitetail, as cited earlier. Blacktails and whitetails are forest deer, period. Any excursions they make into open country are uncommon and not for very long.

The big, gray muley (surprisingly red in summer) is in a class by himself. He's more versatile than the other two — muleys easily adapt either to life in the wide open or in timbered country. Believe it or not, he can outskulk those other two master skulkers. That may raise a lot of eyebrows, but here's the gimmick. In typical whitetail brush and even more so in the thick chaparral or awesome evergreen jungles used by Columbia blacktails, concealment is easy. Just standing still gives a deer near-invisibility much of the time. Muleys in most of their range don't have that luxury. Even their inland western forests are relatively parklike and open. Hiding in open country is yet a harder test. But big muleys do it with astonishing success. A mule deer with a large rack can flatten in sagebrush only thirty inches high and disappear, antlers and all, before the eye of the beholder. I have yet to hunt desert mule deer, but I expect their concealment ability is still better, helped by a surprising amount of both vegetative and terrain cover.

When snow blankets the open hills and rangelands, you'd think the gray of Rocky Mountain mule deer would stand out sharply. Often, it doesn't, because it matches the gray of ever-present sagebrush. The snow-country hunter often has to look hard and use good binoculars to spot mule deer.

Muleys earlier contended with plenty of meat hunters, but mule deer hunting did not become a popular sport in this country until after World War II. These deer had a lot to learn. And they have learned it within just a few decades. Now they're doing postgraduate work in Hunter Avoidance. As Dave Petzal, an experienced hunter, says in the Foreword, the days of big dumb mule deer are gone. The days of big smart muleys are here. The days of even smarter big muleys, you may be sure, are coming. To keep up with them or, we all hope, get ahead, mule deer hunters are going to have to hunt smarter. But let's have a good time doing it, too. This book talks about both of those things.

2

Preparing for the Big Hunt

Guided and unguided hunts have one thing in common. With both, the key to keeping a dream trip from turning into a nightmare lies in planning and preparation, started early and done systematically. These can be a lot of fun in themselves, and the fun can extend for months ahead of the trip.

But if you are thinking of a classic outfitted and guided hunt, do it now. In very recent times, the multiplying cost of liability insurance and the difficulty of just getting such coverage has begun driving even long-established hunting pros out of business. In the better mule deer states, such as Montana, the bulk of professional outfitting may be facing economic extinction due to the liability problem. Except on private ranches, all that may survive are very costly professional services for genuinely wealthy clientele or "guiding" by gas station attendants on their days off.

Assuming some outfitters will still be available for a while, start early to locate a good one. There never were that many — about one licensed guide for every 7,500 American hunters. A year's lead time is not too much to arrange a big, completely outfitted hunt. Picking a capable guide or outfitter for a major hunting trip is a lot more complicated than making an advance motel reservation. Check ads in outdoor magazines, the lists usually provided by state game departments, and additional listings by the "Denali" register of the National Rifle Association. Some taxidermists are good information sources. Even the Chambers of Commerce in some western communities can offer lists of local hunting pros.

When you contact a guide who sounds promising, ask for references. I've never heard of a good pro reluctant to give names of previous clients. Contact them, particularly those who have hunted with him in the last season or two. Do this by phone to question the reference thoroughly. This is the most critical part of planning a guided hunting trip. Also, check with the state game department about the outfitter. They may not know or even be interested in how skilled he is as a hunting guide or whether his camp food is fit to eat. But they should know if he has a track record of angry customers claiming they were shortchanged.

Many guides who arrange only simple, per-day ranch hunts don't go into contractual detail. Bigger outfitters do. Without the hunt terms spelled out in written detail, there can be problems of misunderstanding. A guide-client relationship is like a marriage — it runs best with completely honest two-way communication before getting hitched. Here are items that must be mutually agreed upon by the professional and client:

• How many days are firmly booked? Understand that if you cut short the hunt for any reason, you probably are not entitled to a refund any more than you get a refund from the restaurant for food you ordered but didn't eat.

• How will actual hunting be done — on foot, horseback, or from the bed of a pickup? Will you be camped reasonably close to where you hunt, or spend a couple of nonhunting hours per day on the road?

• How many other hunters will the outfitter have at that time and how many per guide? Get this spelled out in a letter. A party of five, of which I was one, booked with an outfitter who promised we'd be his only hunters that week. Instead, the camp was jammed with twelve; and the hunt was more like NATO war games. Overbooking and resultant overcrowding are terribly common with fly-by-night operators. If your pro overbooks and won't provide some discount or refund for the obviously reduced quality of the hunt, you have a potential mail fraud charge as a bargaining club — *if* you have the booking terms via his letter.

• Who supplies what gear; for instance, must you bring your own saddle scabbard for a horse hunt?

• Insurance coverage — does the outfitter have any? Bear in mind that if *he* gets sued for whatever reason by some third person while he is your contracted agent, *you* might be named in the suit as a codefendant. One outfitter wrecked a costly horse trailer, whose owner then sued both him and the client for whose hunt the trailer had been borrowed.

• Will your guide be hunting simultaneously for himself? If so, who gets the first shot? Once, a guide riding ahead (I'd been given a slow horse and soon knew why) shot the hunt's only bull elk seen inside of five hundred yards. "I needed winter meat," he explained casually.

• What are the house rules about liquor in camp? Some outfitters understandably are not keen on heavy partying by clients; none wants clients drinking while hunting.

• What are the pay terms? Usually an outfitter wants a sizable deposit — typically nonrefundable if you cancel out — at booking, and the balance (cash or check?) at the start (not end) of your hunt.

• Some outfitters keep rates down by having clients help with camp chores. Others for safety reasons *don't* want their pilgrims splitting firewood or helping with the horses. Get this spelled out in advance.

• Aside from the outfitter, how good are the guides themselves? I hunted at one camp where one of the guides killed half a jug every morning, then went into 87-proof hibernation until suppertime. Which was just as well.

• What is expected in the way of tipping guides and camp staff?

• Does your outfitter have any taxidermy tie-in available? If not, is there an extra charge for crating your trophy for shipment?

• What sort of food is offered? Cuisine can range from warmed-up pork-and-beans to good home cooking.

• Will there be any additional fees for extra-good trophies (sometimes assessed not by the guide but by the landowner whose place the guide is leasing)?

One type of outfitting is the drop camp. The hunters have their own camp gear. The outfitter packs them into backcountry and picks them up later. In some areas outfitters are reluctant to do this because they regard on-their-own hunters as less profitable. But where seasons are short, some outfitters think they can make more money servicing a higher number of drop-camp hunters than they can riding herd on fewer full-service clients.

Don't take anything here as an antioutfitter stance. It's a tough way to make a dollar. Although economics may be making them an endangered species in some areas, there are guides and outfitters ranging from good to great. Many guides and customers have developed deep lifelong friendships.

One of my favorite people is Randy Bulkley of Gillette, Wyoming, a hard-working rancher-guide. In his experience, today's clients are often good, sometimes excellent shots. Newcomers to wide-open western hunting sometimes overestimate range and shoot over game. If a hunter has a chronic missing problem, it's likely to be a rifle that changed zero due to getting banged around as luggage enroute. Not surprisingly, some hunters are better stalkers than others, a critical factor in range-country mule deer hunting. Archers are by far the best stalkers, Randy adds.

* * *

Being your own guide-outfitter has advantages. First, some purists feel that they are not hunters but only armed tourists when in the hands of a guide and dependent on his skills. Not to put down guides, mule deer hunting is no unfathomable mystery. I hope you don't need a guide to tell

Expert mule-deer guides like Wyoming's Randy Bulkley (right) know the game, the country, and how to take care of their clients.

The sportsman on his own has more flexibility about when and where to hunt. — *Jackie Nelson Photo*

you the value of hunting fundamentals such as moving upwind, spending more time looking than walking, and using cover.

A distinct advantage of hunting on your own is more flexibility. You can decide when to hunt without being restricted by a guide's booking availability. If you can't make the trip for some reason, no sizable deposit is forfeited. On your own, you decide where, when, how to hunt. In contrast, I once hunted with a Bitterroot guide who refused to try a nearby drainage after the one we pounded six days straight produced no worthwhile game. The explanation was that he was "saving" that other area for his next clients — who scored heavily.

How to pick good hunting country? Information sources are game management people, other sportsmen, forestry personnel, ranchers, farmers, loggers, and rural mail carriers. Off-season scouting for game may be limited by deer using areas that they won't necessarily occupy in late autumn. But it's still a vital help in learning new country. Other things to check on are potential camp sites, what formal campgrounds are still open in fall (many are closed by then), and which back roads may be closed during hunting season.

In scouting an area's hunting potential, keep in mind the mule deer's basic requirements — food and shelter. Water too, since even in desert muley range, any available water is a drawing card. Superadaptable though they are to natural forage, mule deer show great preference for some agricultural crops. Alfalfa, particularly if irrigated, is irresistible. Winter wheat, sown in early fall and in the tender sprout stage by middle and late fall, is another crop that muleys relish. Unless securely fenced, fall-ripening fruit orchards draw deer. But to hold deer, such food hot spots must have cover nearby. In a lot of the no-timber country, cover is in short supply. Any that exists — a low range of rimrock uplands in open range country or the eroded little canyons of a small-scale badlands — is almost certain during the day to shelter resident muleys that feed in open country primarily at night (although less-timid does, fawns, and very young bucks may feed openly in daylight hours).

Timbered mountains are long on shelter and short on good feeding areas. Natural parks or clearings are then likely to cluster mule deer somewhere nearby. In timber country, clearcut areas several years after logging have a wealth of deer-attracting grasses and shrubs except where brush-killing herbicides have been used.

In scouting, taking some notes and making sketch maps can be invaluable later on. One of the niftiest products for this purpose is a waterproof paper for just such outdoors use, made by the J. L. Darling Co., Tacoma, Washington, and sold as note pads in stationery stores.

Although not a substitute for on-the-ground knowledge, thorough map study yields a lot of information. U.S. Geological Survey topographic maps are available in retail locations — my state alone has forty-two retailers stocking USGS maps. Try the Yellow Pages for map retailers. Or write USGS, Federal Center, Denver, Colorado 80225 for an index map from which area maps can be ordered.

A big manager of federal lands is the U.S. Forest Service (USFS). They offer maps of all USFS lands. In addition to smaller offices in or near national forests, USFS western regional offices are the following: Region I, Federal Building, Missoula, Montana 59801; Region II, Building 85, Denver, Colorado 80225; Region III, 517 Gold Avenue, SW, Alburquerque, New Mexico 87101; Region IV, 324–215th Street, Ogden, Utah 84401; Region V, 630 Sansome Street, San Francisco, California 94111; Region VI, Post Office Box 3623, Portland, Oregon 97208.

Not as well known to outdoorsmen is the federal Bureau of Land Management, yet the BLM manages almost twice the acreage that the

USFS does, almost entirely in the West. BLM western regional offices are located in Cheyenne, Wyoming; Salt Lake City, Utah; Portland, Oregon; Santa Fe, New Mexico; Reno, Nevada; Billings, Montana; Boise, Idaho; Denver, Colorado; Sacramento, California; and Phoenix, Arizona.

Some states have extensive forestry holdings for which maps are available either from local state forestry offices or the parent bureau in your state capitol. Maps showing private land ownership are available at county seats. Big timber companies in the U.S. usually open their forest lands to hunting, and some of them offer free maps. The starting point for Canadian maps is the Map Distribution Office, Department of Energy, Mines and Resources, Ottawa, Canada, and provincial capitals where headquarters are located for extensive provincial forestry holdings.

In addition, here's a good tip on the most up-to-date National Forest maps showing latest road construction, fire trails (sometimes not two-wheel-drive passable), and timber harvest clearings. USFS ranger districts frequently update "fireman maps" for their firefighting tactical needs. These are not produced for public distribution. But since new ones must be printed frequently, a district office may have outdated fireman maps that they'll give away. These are still highly useful for hunting purposes, of course, all the more so since such maps show permanent water sources that can be tactically useful hunting information.

Additional maps will be needed because Geographic Survey maps are best in showing unchanging natural terrain. Many of these maps were compiled in the 1950s. Since then, manmade features have changed a great deal — old roads have been abandoned and new roads have been constructed. More updated maps of the kind put out by the Forest Service and other agencies are vital for learning road networks, campgrounds, and other changes.

Good maps show their scale on the margin, expressed as a ratio or fraction; for instance, 1/24,000 means that one inch on the map equals about 24,000 inches or about 2000 feet, close to .4 miles. That is a large-scale map. Some USGS maps run 1/62,500 (1 inch equals nearly a mile), and smaller-scale 1/250,000 or 1/1,000,000 maps. Also on the margin will be a distance scale to help calculate between-points distances. The best way to figure distance on winding roads or trails on maps is with a low-priced map measurer, obtainable at a well-stocked office supply outlet.

What makes a contour map unique are the lines on it that portray the three dimensions of land forms. Contour-line values are shown in the map margin. Let's say the contour interval is eighty feet. A series of four such concentric circles on the map tells you this is an elevation of about 320 feet.

Such a hill on the map may have a small-print datum figure of, say, 4,285. That's 4,285 feet above mean sea level. Our hill is still 320 feet high above lower, flatter land around it. Such information is far more important to the mule deer hunter than is the above-sea-level elevation. That's one reason why it's important to know what contour lines mean.

The contour lines' shape and proximity to each other are keys to understanding the shape of land forms. If our map's eighty-foot contour lines are so close that they're almost touching, they indicate a very steep grade or cliff. Lots of space between contour lines means a gentle slope or almost flat land. A set of contour lines that form a bulge indicate a knob or ridge end. Contour lines forming an acutely angled series of V's indicate a canyon or ravine.

$$* \quad * \quad *$$

Don't try major backcountry penetration by map and compass until you've developed some experience from running simple practice courses by compass. Basic compass and map work is something a fifth grader can learn. That's how old I was when my father taught it to me.

First look on the margin for the "Magnetic North Declination" in the form of a little triangle showing a True North line and, angling off, a Magnetic North line. Your compass, of course, points to Magnetic North, which is somewhere up beyond Hudson's Bay. Compasses in the West are thus off quite a few degrees. In western Washington, for example, the north needle is pointing about twenty-two degrees to the *right* of True North. It will be less for areas farther east.

Even that substantial declination can be ignored for general, knock-about woods hunting. But in a long compass-course hike to hit a small target, allowance must be made for it. To do this properly, you need a compass marked in degrees, not just N/E/S/W. If your map shows a declination of, say, 15 degrees, hold the compass flat and steady, let the North Needle stabilize, and rotate the compass to align the needle with 15 degrees on the dial face that will be east (right) of the circle's 360 degrees (or zero) mark at the top. True North will now be in line with that.

Let's now combine compass and map to get where we want to go. First, put the map on a flat surface — not a motor vehicle's hood, because the metallic mass can cause a compass deviation. Use a straight edge to extend the bottom margin's magnetic declination line right up across the map with a pencil (a pen's line will smear if later dampened from raindrops). This becomes a baseline for Magnetic North when the compass needle is aligned with it. The map is now oriented without further allowance for Magnetic North declination for taking compass-course readings of areas you want to head for.

To get a compass-course reading for hiking off to Buckhorn Mountain, set your compass on your starting point on the map, rotate the compass until the north needle is parallel to the above-described Magnetic North baseline, and use a straight edge (or just your eyesight) to see what the compass bearing would be from starting point to Buckhorn Mountain.

Compass and map work is fun. Some hiking books go into extensive detail on it. In reality, it's all common sense. Keep in mind that often you can't run a straight compass course through the boondocks, since detours may be necessary. When you find that you must detour, take a compass reading on your new course, then take another to get back to approximately the line of travel you were on before detouring. Of course, you have to estimate either by counting paces or keeping track of time (assuming a steady pace) to make sure that both legs of the detour were roughly equal.

But it can be done. The last long compass course I ran was four miles by map in heavily timbered high country. Here I figured out on the map (via the magnetic declination baseline) my primary compass bearing. On the hike, I had to detour around impassable terrain at times. I tried to make detours angular rather than loose half-circles. Then if I counted paces on the detour's first leg, I knew how much to compensate for on the return leg of the detour. Some errors always creep in, of course. Even so, I came out within fifty yards of the rendezvous with my partners.

Early in her hunting career, my wife showed obvious reluctance to believe all this compass jazz. One day I announced to her at breakfast that we'd start at daybreak with a two-hour circle hunt in timber. (Directional changes made no difference, since there was no wind to carry our scent ahead of us.) When we left camp, I took a compass reading, then checked my watch. Every twenty minutes or so, I made a sixty-degree change of course. Since two hours contains six twenty-minute periods, six sixty-degree alterations equalled a full circle.

The good woman was astounded when we exited the forest primeval about thirty yards from where we'd entered. Along with Archimedes, I would have been astounded if we hadn't. Jackie became a true believer in compasscraft; but the main point is that with a compass, simple geometry, and common sense, it's no great trick to keep track of where you are.

Lensatic compasses are made with a folding sighting/bearing reading device for quick, easy readings on distant points. Cheap compasses can be booby traps. In one season, I had three go bad. Two simply had the needles fall off the bearings, and the third reversed polarity to point the north needle permanently south. A good compass is not a big-ticket expense and will last a lifetime.

* * *

Always check your rifle's zero at least before the season's first hunt. First, using properly fitting screwdrivers, check tightness of all scope mount screws *and* the guard screws of a bolt-action rifle. A collimator is a useful device here and in time pays for itself in sight-testing ammunition saved. Even bore-sighting helps when aligning a newly mounted scope, but do it at a minimum of twenty-five yards. Both are approximate at best; the rifle still must be more accurately sighted through live firing.

Two choices exist. One is the time-honored system of getting a shot on target at twenty-five yards, making appropriate scope windage/elevation adjustments, trying another shot, and so on. With the rifle printing on point of aim at twenty-five yards, switch to one hundred and fine tune the adjustments. All firing must be done from as firm a rest as possible to cancel out human aiming errors. The big problem with this system is that it takes lots of ammo and time. Light sporter barrels heat very quickly. Proper sighting-in calls for letting the barrel cool between strings of two or three test shots. Many sporters shoot to different points of impact with hot barrels or cold.

The alternative is called the one-shot system. That's optimistic, but it's still economical of time and ammunition. From a solid rest, fire a carefully aimed shot at one hundred yards (assuming the rifle is sighted at least well enough to print on paper at that range — otherwise, start in at twenty-five or fifty yards). Next, walk down to the target and very plainly mark that bullet hole with a grease pencil if it's in the white or a small white paper patch if in the black, all this so you can see it in your rifle scope.

Aim again at the center of the target. Now comes the tricky part. By use of sand bags or whatever, get the rifle firmly anchored. If nothing else, have a companion stand beside you to hold it in place by brute force. Gently adjust the scope to bring the crosshairs on to your well-marked bullet hole. All this time, the rifle must be held firmly positioned in its original, aimed-at-target-center position. A padded vise would be ideal, but that's hard to arrange at a shooting bench.

If done right, you align the crosshairs with the demonstrated point of impact of the rifle. If you manage to jiggle the rifle before moving the crosshairs to where they should be, start again with another test shot, then go on from there. Once you do get the rifle on point of aim at one hundred yards, do some conventional test shots coupled with a bit of elevation increase to make it print about 1¾ inches to 2 inches high at one hundred yards with a cool barrel. With typical modern deer loads (270/ 130 grain, 30–06/150 grain), that will put you right on point of aim at two hundred yards, or mighty close to it. The reasons for this are spelled out in Chapter 6.

Some chaps sight to print even higher at one hundred yards in order to extend point-of-aim/impact to 250 yards or so. Unless you kill all your deer at three hundred-plus yards, that's too much of a good thing. The problem with sighting in at too long a range is that you have an increasingly high midrange trajectory—that is, the bullet will be printing perhaps three inches high halfway to your on-aim range. Since it's all too easy to miss game by hurried overshooting, let's not compound the felony by sighting in for too high a midrange trajectory.

After sighting in precisely, oiling the barrel is a question. The problem is that many rifles shoot off point of aim with the first shot from a heavily oiled barrel. If your first shot is at game, that's not good. My choice is to run a very lightly oiled patch a couple of times through the bore, then case the rifle for the trip. If you thoroughly clean and oil the bore, fire a fouling shot somewhere to blow out the goop before you get to your hunting country.

When packing to travel, put your rifle in a stout case, and do *not* pack it under heavy gear in your motor vehicle. Don't have it in plain view, either, to incite a fast theft when you're in the gas station men's room. If flying commercial air, it had better be a strong case to take the usual luggage bashing. When booking a hunting trip flight, it's wise to check first to make sure a particular airline accepts properly luggaged firearms.

Sometimes airlines lose or delay luggage, including cased guns, which can naturally foul up your whole trip. One thoughtful hunter I know ships a spare rifle two weeks ahead of time to his outfitter. If his main rifle gets lost in the air terminal shuffle, he's still ready to hunt with a familiar rifle rather than a hand-me-down spare of the outfitter's.

3

Boots and Clothes for the Mule Deer Hunter

About to fall to certain death, I found my feeling of pure terror was momentarily overridden by anger. If I hadn't been stupid about my footwear on this mountain hunting trip, I wouldn't be in this pickle — sliding very slowly but surely down a sloping rock face from whose edge I would drop one hundred feet to jagged talus like dragon's teeth below. After surviving World War II and pneumonia in the preantibiotic days, what a rotten way to go.

Just then a tense voice said "Grab it." It came from my teenage son, who I didn't know was even near. He had his rifle barrel stuck out as far as possible. I could barely reach it with one hand. For a couple of seconds my life depended on that slender, oily tube. With neither of us daring to breathe, he slowly pulled me up to where I got one of my treacherous boot soles planted in the same rock fissure that gave him firm footing. Then I took a long breath and decided never again to hunt steep country without lug-sole boots. I've spent a heap of spare time staying off smooth rock since then, too.

What almost did me in was a pair of bird boots with flat crepe soles. They had carried me many a mile comfortably and quietly in flatland grouse and deer hunting. But the crepe soles gave poor purchase on mountain slopes because of their worn-slick surface and lack of heel indentation. That's what got me into trouble when I tried to traverse the rock face with its deceptively gentle slope.

That incident years ago on my first high country muley hunt made me a footwear fanatic. But even without such clifftop trauma, think it over: Footwear is the most important part of your hunting gear. Yea verily, more so than a Dave Gentry custom mountain rifle and Zeiss binoculars. Fat lot of good they are if improper footgear has you camp-bound with severe blisters, a torn ligament, or learning to use a hospital bedpan with a shattered leg in traction. In the final crunch, your feet are what take you hunting. Nowhere is this more true than in mule deer hunting with its often formidable rugged distances.

Basically there are four types of footgear demands to be considered by the mule deer hunter. These are: 1) use in very rough terrain, typically with lots of rock and other bad footing; 2) quieter walking or energy-saving use on easier ground; 3) safe use in saddle stirrups; 4) wear in wet or cold conditions. The best any single type of footwear can do is two of these jobs — none handle all four tasks.

In steep country, the boots must be both high *and* stiff enough to provide good ankle support, or you'll be very sorry, believe me. Not only sore-ankled-sorry but possibly stranded in a high and hostile environment with an immobilizing sprain. That can be a life-threatening situation. Boots stout enough for good ankle support are: 1) made of leather, since fabric-upper boots are too supple; and 2) fairly stiff leather in the bargain — not soft glovelike uppers. Such boots tend to be heavy by today's standards, particularly when compared to the trendy, very light footwear beloved by Granola Set hikers. Their lightweights are fine for summer hiking on established trails or moderate grades. Some of them make good, quiet "stalking feet." But such low hiking shoes lack support for tougher work on steep no-trail slopes.

Long ago I learned that the Bluebird of Happiness for the serious muley hunter is to have two sets of footwear on a trip. My basic boots are stiff-ankled, lug-soled jobs for tough terrain. But I also bring along a pair of lighter boots. Which ones depends on where I'm hunting. One choice has softer composition soles and well-defined heels — if not crepe rubber, something similar. Those are for wear in moderate terrain such as the low hills and little badlands of typical Great Plains mule deer country.

An alternative pair are fabric (apparently nylon) hiking shoes. These offer little ankle support and give me wet feet if I so much as sneeze heavily. But they're great for prowling easier terrain more quietly than heavy boots permit. Wearing these lightweights, I sure stay away from

Even in gentler terrain, lug soles are important if you plan to climb up on logs, stumps, or rocks to see better.

prickly pear and have no illusions about them stopping the strike of even a small short-fanged rattler — let alone a forty-six-inch Montana timber rattler like one that guide-outfitter Pat McFall and I civilized with an entrenching tool near Pat's mountain cabin. Even so, these are useful hunting shoes — light, comfortable, and almost moccasin-quiet. They're also great to slip into with a sigh of relief after bigger, heavier boots are removed from my high-mileage, hot, tired feet back in camp.

For wet-snow hunting, shoepacks (leather uppers, rubber lowers) with good lug soles are essential. A truly waterproof all-leather boot is like a perpetual motion machine — a splendid idea but still a dream. The porosity of leather makes it impossible for that wonderful material to be rendered water-impervious. All the more so when seams leak too. Most of my life I have hunted in leather boots a great deal and have tried *every* boot-waterproofing substance — oil, grease, wax compounds, and silicon. The best any of them will do is keep out a heavy dew and then only for a few hours. That's not really waterproof.

Hence the need for shoepacks for snow hunting. Not that they're the perfect solution. To date, I have not found shoepacks with the ankle support of firm all-leather boots. In wet snow, feet will stay drier in shoepacks, which is critically important. For anything hillier than a supermarket parking lot, shoepacks must be lug-soled. Alas, these are much noiser. But smoother-bottomed packs will spill you so fast on *any* slope that you'll think it was a hit and run accident. Again, that's something I learned the hard way more than once.

For real cold, shoepacks big enough to take felt liners are better. Even so, you can get cold or possibly frostbitten feet. I've often hunted in minus-twenty-degree weather, which is a great incentive to experiment for warmer footgear. Long ago I gave up on the insulated rubber "Korean boots." They're not all that warm and about as clumsy as wearing cement sandals. Some years back, military surplus boots of hard felt with buckle-up canvas uppers were on the market. These were made with a huge last to permit multiple pairs of socks plus double layers of thick felt insoles. Although warm, their hard composition soles are hopelessly slippery. To beat this rap, I stapled and glued lateral cleats of rubber weatherstripping on the soles. This not only provides good traction but allows quiet walking on rocks or other hard surfaces.

The northern Rockies are no Garden of Eden in late November, and anyone who hunted this region at that time in 1985 will recall bone-chilling cold. My son and I were working the foothills country north of Spokane, Washington, which is grab-bag hunting — either muleys or whitetails — in temperatures that got down to twenty-two below on

Thanksgiving Day. However, that hunt was a milestone for me — it was the first time I hunted weather that frigid without getting cold feet. The secret was my footwear. No boots. Instead, a pair of oversized dress overshoes that contained felt insoles. On my feet from the skin out were polypropylene socks, two pairs of thick wool socks, and a pair of felt booties. We were afoot in eighteen inches of snow, so I made a pair of gaiters to seal snow out of the tops of the overshoes. Actually this footwear was pretty good for walking if I didn't attempt steep grades. They also had the virtue of quietness. Ankle support was not great; but the snow had driven both deer and hunters out of the high and rugged into gentler foothills.

For horseback riding, any of the boots cited above can work if they are stirrup-safe. This is literally a life and death matter. Here's why. The reason classic cowboy boots have those narrow toes and high heels is not to look cute dancing the fandango. The sharp taper slides out easily out of stirrups. The prominent heel makes it impossible to slip the foot all the way into the stirrup. All this because the potentially deadliest thing to happen to a rider is to get his foot through a stirrup. Then if he loses his seat or (maybe more likely) falls when dismounting, he can be held by the ankle and dragged. Usually a hapless rider in that situation is dead within one hundred yards if the horse, spooked by all this commotion, starts running.

Therefore, pointy-toed, high-heeled boots are for safety in riding. Unfortunately, such boots are no good for anything else. Even sheathed in the formfit overshoes sold in the West for cowboy boots, they're cold to the toes and miserable to walk any distance. Thus, many horseback hunters use more acceptable hunting footwear as de facto riding boots. But such boots *must* slip out easily from the stirrup. Here, the trusty lug sole can be fatal if it snags in the stirrup in dismounting and manages to suspend you with your noggin under the hind hooves of a excited horse. That can lead to you being known posthumously as the Headless Horseman.

If you have a small foot, be careful, because then your boots may be capable of slipping through the stirrups. Boots too big can get wedged in too-small stirrups. Many western hunting riders and outfitters use "winter stirrups," which are oversized to let big hunting boots slip back out easily.

If you're riding an outfitter's horse, check your boot and stirrup fit carefully, since it's your neck at risk. If there's a problem, call it to your outfitter's attention so that he can change stirrups. Just make sure at all times that you keep your feet only partly into the stirrups to allow them to slip free in case of a fall by you or the horse.

Warm weather or cold, wear some type of insoles in your boots.

Even the thin sponge-rubber ones sold in drugstores are foot savers. Thicker felt insoles greatly improve foot warmth. An overlooked fringe benefit of insoles is that they extend sock life.

Even in warm weather, the thicker and more cushiony your socks, the more mileage your feet will take. If your boots are oversize, extra socks or insoles are vital to prevent your feet from sliding inside them. That's a quick way to develop crippling blisters, even more so going downhill. Uphill travel is hard on your legs. Sidehill travel taxes the ankles. Downhill hammers the feet.

For cold weather, wool socks are best, but a pair of polypropylene socks next to the skin helps foot warmth by wicking away foot perspiration. While quality wool socks aren't cheap, the costliest socks are the cheapos that may not last even one hunting trip. A percentage of synthetics like nylon or orlon strengthens wool socks. Still, the thickest, warmest socks are all wool. Don't wear so many socks that your feet have to jamfit into your boots. That restricts circulation and guarantees cold feet. If you do a lot of hunting in cold weather, consider buying a spare pair of oversize boots to allow thicker insoles plus extra socks.

Down-filled booties are a farce for foot-warming. Down is effective insulation only when it maintains some fluffiness (called "loft") for trapping dead air pockets. Down booties worn on the feet get squeezed by too much pressure to maintain loft. They make nice camp slippers; that's all.

The jury still seems to be out on the question of electrically heated socks. I have not used them myself, and I hear them equally praised or damned by those who have. My main objection is that I usually have plenty of gear to carry without adding a set of batteries. Often on the move, which helps keep feet warm, a muley hunter with any common sense in sock and boot choice shouldn't need heated socks. However, they might be a good idea for horseback hunting in cold weather. Battery weight then is no problem, and feet do get cold when you're in the saddle long periods without walking. Heated socks also may be worthwhile for wintry stump-sits on muley migration trails.

*   *   *

The key element in western hunting is the extreme temperature range possible in the fall. Many times I have arisen before daybreak to thaw a coffee pot of solid ice on the camp stove, thanks to a nighttime low of fifteen to eighteen degrees. Yet 11:00 A.M. the same October day might see ninety degrees, meaning a temperature range of seventy to eighty degrees in only six hours. And *next* day could bring a wicked cold front with icy rain or several inches of snow even at lower elevations. As the hackneyed saying goes in the West, if you don't like the weather, just wait fifteen minutes, when it will surely change.

Naturally, this poses problems in dressing for mule deer hunting. The wise hunter must be prepared for both extremes. That means light clothes — jeans and short-sleeved shirt — plus spare clothes warm enough for below-freezing weather, quite likely with cold winds that do dismaying things to wind-chill factors. For example, a mild temperature of fifty-five and a thirty mph wind produces a wind-chill factor of twenty-eight degrees, in effect, almost thirty degrees under the thermometer reading.

Dressing for hot weather is simple. Cotton is the ticket here. A light ventilated cap with a good long visor is okay for hot weather use, although it's not the sunshield that a lightweight hat is. Antisunburn tip for hot weather hunting: Anchor a bandanna from the cap's rear band to hand down over the back of your neck, Foreign Legion kepi style. (And if anyone calls you Beau Geste, you know which salute to give 'em.)

Back in the 1950s, when easterners in numbers first took up muley hunting, many good Michiganders and Pennsylvanians could be seen miserable in their wool shirts and heavy Malone wool britches in ninety-degree weather. First trip West, they didn't know any better. To them, deer hunting usually meant cold weather. At least they had the excuse of first-trip ignorance. For my money, native westerners are the slow learners when it comes to dressing properly. Often I've seen locals turning blue with chattering teeth, thanks to their obsession with light jeans and flannel shirts in wool-and-raingear weather.

Sometimes this lack of foresight kills them. Several years ago I was hunting elk in mild coastal Washington when a storm roared in with three days of steady rain and wind. The temperature never went below fifty-five degrees, but with a wind velocity of forty to sixty knots, you're looking at a wind chill factor in the twenties or lower. A teenage hunter in our area got lost late in the afternoon of the storm's first day. Without warm clothes or raingear, he was found dead of hypothermia, and probably died that first night.

The great misunderstanding is that weather well above freezing may be uncomfortable but not life threatening. Wrong! Plenty of people have died of hypothermia in air temperatures in the fifties. Some years back, three contestants in an English walking race perished this way, thanks to wet cotton clothing that sucks away heat *240* times faster than dry cotton. That drains your body heat quicker than your metabolism can replace it. This sets the stage for hypothermia. More on this in Chapter 15.

For cool-to-cold weather hunting garb, here are the basics:

• Have long underwear available, either waffle-weave cotton thermal type, woolen, or insulated, depending on weather. As with socks, a layer of moisture-absorbing polypropylene underwear next to the skin (with other longies over that) is highly effective in really cold weather. Real insulated underwear is too warm for an active wearer doing lots of hill climbing but is great stuff if you're inactive (riding a horse, trail-watching) at lower temperatures.

• Wool and flannel are typical hunting-shirt materials. Flannel, remember, is only fluffed cotton and useless for warmth if wet. Two medium shirts are better than one thick shirt, because the layer between them is dead-air insulation — the so-called layered principle. Also, with two shirts on, you have the option of shucking one as the day warms or you become heated going uphill.

• A medium-weight wool hunting jacket is essential for cool and cold-weather hunting and has surprising water repellency, all the more if treated with silicone spray sold for that purpose. This jacket should be roomy enough to allow a down vest or heavy sweater underneath. Wool is also the quietest material, which is important to the big-game hunter.

• Rain garment choices range from cheap vinyl to better, costlier nylon, coated with rubber or plastic. The cheapos are light and compact to carry but can be torn to confetti in one day of timber hunting. Ponchos offer plenty of rain, snow, and wind protection. However, they're noisy, hamper fast rifle handling, and are no good in timber. I once drew a horse from an outfitter's string who was docile until I put on a poncho. That garment flapping in the wind scared her into lunacy.

• Except when you're sure of hot weather, trousers should be wool. Unfortunately, *light* wool hunting britches are almost impossible to buy. Consider dedicating a pair of old dress trousers for this purpose if they're not dangerously game-imitative gray or light brown. Twills are the strongest weave but much noisier than softer wools.

• Down garments are famed for warmth — when dry and fluffy. Wet and matted, they're useless.

• Windbreakers made of nylon are useful, and when treated for water repellency can partially substitute for rain gear. But nylon's rustling noise is in the high-frequency range that animals hear far better than we do. For timber hunting, you might just as well wear a cowbell to announce your approach.

• A hunter always faces a hard choice between maximum hand warmth (mittens) and finger dexterity (gloves). Good wool gloves are adequate to about ten degrees Fahrenheit. Below that, mitts may be necessary to keep your fingers usable. Trigger-finger mitts are usually too thick for most trigger guards and can cause an accidental shot, heaven forbid. Lined leather gloves aren't good below freezing. Cotton gloves are hopeless except in temperatures warm enough not to require gloves.

Thick, insulated mitts popular with skiers and snowmobilers take much longer to slip off than looser mitts.

• A thick wool scarf is a heat preserver out of all proportion to its modest size, weight, and cost. It acts as a sealing gasket around your neck to keep body heat from escaping. In cold weather it can save your ears from frostbite.

• The classic western cowboy hat not only provides some portable shade in a land of fierce sun but also is better than a cap to keep rain and snow out of the back of your neck. Get it big enough to stay on well in the wind. The big disadvantages are that it's a twig-plunking nuisance when you're trying to quietly still-hunt timber, and it provides no ear protection.

• Paraphrasing the long-ago politician who said that what the country really needed was a good five-cent cigar, what northern tier hunters need today is a good wool cap. These have become hard to find. The vinyl abortions available are noisemakers in the brush. For real cold, a trooper-style cap with fold-down earflaps is excellent. Knitted wool caps are warm when thick enough, but many are skimpy. Caps without bills or visors offer no snow or rain protection to your face, eyes, or glasses.

In all the cold weather hunting I've done, I've been overheated far more often that I've been cold. Even so, I stuff a down jacket or vest in my daypack facing a cold day ahead — just in case. The vital thing is to stay dry. Your body is quite a furnace if it's not sabotaged by wet garments sucking out the heat. Thus, waterproof or water repellent outer garments can be more important than, say, a moisture-vulnerable down jacket that quickly loses insulative value in rain or falling snow.

One more thing. If you begin a hunt in cold weather, you'll find that you acclimatize quickly. By Day 2, you're wearing less as your heat regulatory system changes gears to adapt to the colder environment. But, some extra garb in daypack or saddlebags is playing it smart.

4

Happy Hunting Camps

"Hunting camp" years ago implied either a tent camp or a fixed base such as a cabin. Today a hunting camp can be anything from a shell canopy on a minipickup to a bus-sized motor home. Yet tent camping is still around and has undergone a rebirth of sorts. Which is the best system for mule deer hunting in the West? Some hunters simply buy a recreational vehicle, then let *it* decide where they'll hunt—there is no backroad use with a big motor home. But it makes more sense to decide on a mode of hunting camp based on your style of hunting, where you hunt, how ambitious you are, and how big your hunting budget is. Remember that in many places recreational vehicles and/or tents can be rented.

If most of your hunting is within two to three hours of home, do you really need a substantial recreational vehicle with space for prolonged hunts? If you hunt rugged country, can you safely and conveniently expect to get a big truck camper or trailer in and out of it? When I acquired a new cabover truck camper, the first thing I learned was that the overhang of timber on narrow forest roads could tear the fragile aluminum camper skin towering well above the truck cab. If your party scores on both deer and heavy elk, how do you expect to haul home maybe one thousand pounds of game when already the camper, gear, human occupants, and fuel load have your rig loaded at or over maximum tire capacity?

What's the size of your hunting party? A shell canopy on even a big pickup is adequate for only two people. Do not expect the rated sleeping capacity of any recreational vehicle to be realistic when used for hunting. Big cabover campers may have sleeping space for six adults, but only under ideal conditions, such as warm-weather vacationing. Four wet, weary hunters and their spare gear crammed into a pickup camper are too many; they are always in each other's way changing clothes, trying to dry wet clothes, and cooking and eating meals. Such overcrowding is okay if everyone is tolerant, avoids bringing too much personal gear, and "keeps house" meticulously. Certainly it's tolerable over a weekend. But it can be sheer temper-fraying misery on a week-long hunt, particularly if bad weather requires clothes drying and rules out storage of gear outside.

With such realities in mind, let's look at the features of today's recreational vehicles.

TRUCK CAMPERS — These include four basic types. First is the simple shell canopy, either homemade or purchased new for a few hun-

Pickup loses little or no mobility with installation of a low, shell canopy, but obviously little space is available for vehicle camping.

dred dollars. It's light and has plenty of capacity for equipment and hauling deer carcasses. It lacks comfort space, although two can spike-camp it okay.

Second is the bigger slide-in truck camper, usually with cab overhang space. New models cost several thousand dollars. Second-hand jobs can often be acquired for a few hundred on up. Included are a gas stove with oven, and some refrigeration space (which may be only an ice box). Optional are toilets and gas furnaces. These campers definitely require beefed-up trucks of the ¾-ton variety, and the heaviest-rated tires you can find. Even then, a truck camper has some serious driving limitations. The big ten-foot models have lots of rear overhang, less ability to handle poor roads, and are no fun to drive in severe winds. But they will accommodate three hunters. A great virtue of these campers is that on long nonstop trips the off-duty watch can get real rest in a genuine bed before taking a turn at the wheel.

The third style is the big, chassis-mounted camper, often on a ton-rated truck. Closely related are the mini-motor homes built on van-type chassis. For both, the advantages are more living comfort and storage space—not to be confused with extra cargo-weight capacity, which often they don't have. Disadvantages are that these are not for serious off-road travel or narrow forest roads. Dual rear tires on most of these jobs can be treacherous for skidding on ice and snow due to their reduced load-bearing area.

The fourth type includes the van-body campers that, unlike the ones cited above, retain most of the original body. They range from minis like the popular Volkswagen van line, on up to ¾-ton models. Vans with removable seats can double as campers similar in space to a shell canopy on a pickup truck. Cooking can be done on a gas stove, sleeping on floor mattresses. Other vans are rebuilt internally as true campers with built-in stoves, cabinets, and sinks. Some have raised roofs, either fixed or pop-up, for standing room.

BIG MOTOR HOMES — A class in themselves, these bus-sized rigs are the last word in sheer comfort, but are not necessarily good for hunting. They're pretty much for paved roads only; one model I measured had only six inches of under clearance. Their plush, doll-house interiors do not go well with rough-and-muddy hunting use. Lots of space goes into luxuries such as bathtubs and built-in vanity tables. But if you want deluxe safaris including (with some) built-in 110V power, they have it—for a price typically exceeding thirty thousand dollars.

TENT TRAILERS — Light and relatively low-priced, these have been refined steadily over the years by such companies as Coleman. Some are composites, part tenting, part aluminum. Thanks to their lightness and low profile for bucking headwinds and side sway, they're towable by smaller vehicles even on steep grades. Although too wide for some narrow forest roads, they don't have the tree-limb-vulnerable height of most recreational vehicles. Because of their large screened "window" styling, they're the best of non-air-conditioned recreational rigs for hot weather camping.

Drawbacks include put-up and take-down time and lack of weather-tightness in chilly, windy weather. With good heaters, they can be used more in colder weather than many people realize. Due to their limitations of living and storage space, consider these as two-to-three-hunter rigs regardless of extra sleeping room.

TRAVEL TRAILERS — This covers trailers from thirteen feet on up. Mini trailers are based originally on European designs and are good two-person outfits. Bigger models at most are four-hunter units. A recent variant is the fifth-wheel trailer designed to be tow-connected inside the bed of a pickup for better roadability.

Travel trailers generally offer much more room than truck campers. For one thing, some spare gear can be stored in the tow vehicle. Only the larger chassis campers and motor homes compare to the living and storage space of even medium-sized vacation trailers. Small-to-medium trailers are less problem to tow on open highways than many novices expect. Trailers can be a problem in strong headwinds or when traction is bad on snow, ice, or mud. Learning to back into a predetermined spot is not hard but requires some practice. Larger models require independent braking controls (regulations vary by state). For trailer towing in warm weather and steep country, a towing vehicle with special transmission cooling and oversize radiator, either as a factory "towing package" option or retro-fitted, is strongly recommended.

No vacation trailer should be towed with a simple bumper hitch. Frame-mounted equalizing hitches are vital. (In theory, such hitch systems reduce vehicle clearance and should make it easier to get stuck. In reality, that rarely happens. High-centering of the front running gear or transmission housing is the usual problem.)

From the hunting standpoint, a vacation trailer offers many advantages. Detached and used as a base camp, it frees the towing vehicle for more arduous use on roads not suitable for a truck camper or van camper. One tactical advantage is that the party can split their efforts — some operating on foot from the trailer camp for the day, while others take the vehicle to hunt some more distant area. When used in non-reserved sites, the parked trailer holds your camping space when you and your vehicle are elsewhere. That can be crucial where pull-off spots both large and level enough are scarce — a common problem in many mountain areas.

If you hunt one area several times during the season, maybe a trailer can be left at a friend's home nearby, so that you can commute back and forth "running light." This saves fuel, vehicle wear and tear, and is an obvious advantage in crossing mountains, particularly in dubious weather. True, a slip-off truck camper can be left to tie down camping space or for next-weekend use. But in real life, camper owners use this take-off feature less and less with the passage of time because it's a real hassle with any jacking system.

Whatever your choice, give serious thought to fittings and accessories. In freezing weather, a toilet can't be used without lacing the holding tank with plenty of expensive antifreeze. A shower means an added drain on water supply if you're sited far from convenient hose-filling sources, and also burns up a surprising amount of LP gas. If a water heater is used, it must be kept going at all times in cold weather to avoid freezing the system.

Since most western hunting is done in occasionally chilly or downright frigid weather, a heating system is essential in any camping rig. Built-in gas furnaces in subzero weather may need help from portable catalytic heaters. Always make sure you're getting sufficient ventilation with any heating system, and do *not* use monoxide-generating blue-flame stove heat for heating purposes. Choosing between an ice box or a gasfired refrigerator depends again on your likely mode of use. A vertically mounted RV ice box is not as efficient as a chest cooler and will need ice replenishment in two to three days unless weather is cold.

In my decades of western hunting, I've used various recreational vehicle systems in everything from far-below-zero weather to burning heat. The system I ended up with is twofold. On my 4wd pickup, I keep a homemade canopy with a flip-top roof to provide spacious standing room. It has slide-out bed space for two and built-in cabinets for an LP camp stove and food storage. This spike camp on wheels is comfortable for short hunts involving two persons. I also use a low-priced (no toilet) sixteen-foot travel trailer for longer base-camp hunts, particularly in cold weather.

Good tip: If you have a non-trailer recreational vehicle, shop around for insurance. Some underwriters offer fifty percent discounts on campers — defined as a self-propelled unit (no trailers) with built-in cooking and sleeping systems.

*   *   *

One reason for the comeback of tent camping by hunters is that a quality tent and all the camp gear needed cost only a fraction of the outlay for various motor-camping systems, not counting insurance and depreciation.

Despite the RV revolution, tent camping has made a comeback in recent years. A tent is the ultimate in back-to-nature outdoors living with the sights and sounds of nature. And only a big motor home can match a sizable tent for living space.

Relatively low cost is another reason for tent camping's popularity. You can outfit lavishly with a top-of-the-line tent and all the camp gear you need for only a fraction of a motor camper's cost. Durability? A tent with reasonable care will outlast the tin tepees! In the early 1950s I bought a budget-priced nine-by-twelve-foot canvas wall tent. Although I later bought other tents, that one is still going strong, albeit with good care and some maintenance over the years. Since I paid $50 for it, it's cost me about $1.50 a year to own it. Just sitting in the driveway, a truck camper costs much more than that *per day* for insurance and depreciation, not counting maintenance.

From the confusing array of tents today, selecting one requires thinking about your present and future needs. Obey two important rules. First, don't go by price alone. Second, when in doubt about tent size, always get the next larger model.

Tent material is a crucial question. Cotton tenting ranges from heavy duck to light poplin. Cotton is fairly strong and breathes well to prevent internal condensation. Nylon is stronger, mildew-resistant, and can be made more waterproof than cotton. The newest tent materials are synthetics, like Kimberly Clark's polypropylene fabric called *Evolution 3*. This achieves waterproof integrity along with ability to breathe, while having nylon's resistance to mildew and organic rot—both killers of cotton. It's also surprisingly light. The relatively thick fluffiness of polypropylene tenting may have better insulative qualities. However, it does not appear as strong as cotton or nylon.

Skipping small tents for backpack hunting (covered in Chapter 11), first take a look at the intermediate-sized tents for three or more persons. These tents come in a variety of designs from the traditional A-style to panel-sided igloo models. Still others resemble the half-tubular design of covered wagons. One classic is the umbrella tent, originally designed for a center pole but nowadays using external frames. The old tried-and-true Whelen, Baker, and Forester designs seen in any camping book are still with us for good reason. As a rule, tents of more conventional designs cost less than more exotic models of approximately the same quality. For a base camp tent, consider a 9 x 12 or an equivalent 100 to 110 square-foot model as a minimum for four hunters, better with only three, ideal for two.

In the big-tent category, the smallest are actually oversized umbrella tents, the largest are A-roof styles with either vertical or sloped walls. Design variations include my big Winnebago Chieftain IV which is shed-like—highest in the middle, slightly lower fore and aft. This design provides more head room than standard A-shaped roofs. Its drawback is that it lacks enough pitch to shed snow. The big wall tents used by outfitters are still available from custom-tent makers. My son's has a roomy 168 square feet, but that's dwarfed by a hunting partner's 14 x 20 model with 280 square feet.

An extended, all-weather camp for several hunters takes lots of tent. My Winnebago's ten-by-sixteen dimensions exceed the average bedroom. But now consider moving four people into that bedroom along with spare gear, cots, cooking stove and table, plus a heating stove. Things get crowded quickly. Actually, even this ten-by-sixteen tent is best for only three hunters. Double-decker camp cots help the tent-space situation greatly.

One way to beat the space crunch is to rig a tented annex or porch at the front entry, using large tarps or plastic sheeting, then do the cooking in this, which helps keep the tent cool in hot weather. Even a small wood stove heats a large tent well in cold weather, but wood consumption will be high. The stovepipe is best run through a slit in a wall seam; and be sure to use a heat-baffling system to avoid scorching or setting fire to the tent.

Outfitter tents have no windows, but get plenty of illumination through the white canvas roof. Family tents designed for summertime camping have lots of screened window area. However, they can be warm enough for cold weather when zipped up and a heating system is in use. If you are buying an LP catalytic heater for tent use, pick the highest BTU-heat-output model available.

One important warning about cold weather tenting: Heavy snow wrecks the exterior frames typical of family tents. Except for southwestern desert hunting, snow is always an autumn possibility. This is a strong argument for a conventional outfitter's tent that is designed to be erected with stout cut-sapling poles and can handle snow better.

Outfitter tents usually are made without floors. That keeps weight down. You won't miss a floor unless camping in bad insect weather or in areas with snake problems. Some campers spread a large tarp as a floor. But even in snow camping that's not essential. Believe it or not, a moderate amount of snow underfoot in a floorless tent quickly packs down hard and smooth as linoleum and is easy to sweep clean! Stove heat won't melt it except right next to the stove. Some hunters bring baled hay to spread atop snow in a floorless tent. But that's a terrific mess and a serious fire hazard. The better floorless tents are made with a sod cloth. That's simply a lower wall extension to be tucked under an inside floor tarp to eliminate floor drafts. Banking with snow, pine needles, or leaves will help, too. Needless to say, a cot and good sleeping pad beat sleeping on the floor of any tent, all the more in a floorless model.

When buying a tent, look closely at the quality of zippers, seam stitching, and frame or pole fittings. Grommets and loops deserve close examination. Check any rope work. Cheap tents use low-grade lines that should be replaced before first use.

Other tent tips:

• Always be fire conscious. Keep an extinguisher in the tent. Do all gasoline refueling outside for safety and because spilled fuel is hard on tent floors.

• Pack spare tent pegs and extra cordage for extra tie-downs in cold weather.

• A new cotton tent needs at least one, and preferably two, thorough wet-downs and dry-outs at home to shrink material to waterproof it. Nylon and other synthetics such as Evolution 3 are likely to leak in seams when new and require seam sealant application.

• Never put a tent away damp. Spread it out or hang it to dry. Never store a tent on a concrete floor.

• When camping on public lands, check beforehand about campfire or wood-cutting permits.

• No tentmaker yet has had wit enough to install interior loops from which clothes-drying and lantern-hanging line can be safely rigged. Yet no tent should be without these. Get such loops installed even if takes a trip to the local tent-and-awning shop.

*   *   *

More important than what you camp in is how you run a hunting camp. This affects not only the pleasure of the hunt but even the likelihood of getting game.

First, plan your travel fuel logistics, because finding all-night gas service in thinly populated areas is a real problem. A long trip to go hunting can be shortened by eating sandwiches en route. Each time you stop to eat, your lose from thirty to fifty miles of driving time. If you opt for a restaurant meal, pick a truck stop—these have faster service.

Plan your camp's operation to save time. In the short days of November and December, you have only about 540 minutes of daylight—less in northern latitudes. Time spent on camp chores shooteth no game. Nothing saves more camp time than fast meal preparation. When packing food for a hunt of several days, I put each meal's provisions into paper sacks marked 1, 2, or 3, denoting breakfast, lunch, or dinner. These in turn go into the main grub box. Ice cooler provisions like meats are also coded for day and meal. Thus no time is lost rummaging around for random food and head-scratching about what to fix for a particular meal. This also helps you get a firm handle on actual grub requirements, avoiding the common problem of bringing too much (a nuisance) or bringing too little (a disaster).

A camp stove far surpasses a wood fire for speed of meal preparation. Pick foods for minimum prep time. Instant rice takes one-fourth the cooking time of conventional rice. Dehydrated potatoes are far faster than peeling and boiling raw spuds. Sausage and cheese are protein substitutes for fresh meats, which must be cooked. Instant coffee is faster than regular java. If an oven is available, scorn not the lowly TV dinner for speed, convenience, and minimum wash up. Save breakfast time by cooking bacon the night before, then warming it next morning as the eggs are frying. Eat perishable foods like hamburger early in the hunt. Pre-cooked meals (casseroles, fried chicken) can be brought from home to reduce meal preparation time on the first day or two of camping. Just be careful of quick-spoiling foods like potato salad.

Use of disposable plates and utensils saves dishwashing time and cuts down on water consumption. These steps also save cooking fuel, another time saver when firewood must be cut and split. The noon meal is the one that burns up hunting daylight, assuming you breakfast before sunup and have dinner at day's end. Plan fast, easy lunches — sardines, cold meats, canned fruits, bread.

What about garbage handling? *No* place is remote enough to casu-ally dump your refuse. Bring plenty of plastic garbage sacks, use them, and be man enough to haul them out when you drive home. For human wastes, dig a latrine pit, using the earthen spoil to cover each deposit — remember that flies drawn there will be around your foodstuffs shortly. Although I can rough it along with anyone, I cherish a neat camp toilet, complete with a portable seat, as a touch of high-class campcraft, not to mention comfort. Toilet paper in a waterproof tin can, please.

In a master trip-planning conference, get agreement on menus. Let him who can't stand oatmeal speak now or forever shut his trap. This is the time to thrash out who does the cooking, how to finance groceries, and other trip expenses. A common system is for everyone to chip in to a master slush fund that will be used to buy everything from gas to gro-ceries. Liquor is best privately stocked, since nondrinkers can't be ex-pected to help pay for it. Likewise, anyone with offbeat food tastes — like me with my buttermilk — should buy those on his own.

*   *   *

The following is a deliberately long, pick-and-choose list of items to consider for a major hunting trip. It can be pruned to meet your needs and in fact would have to be reduced drastically for a pack-string trip or backpack hunt.

GENERAL GEAR FOR ANY HUNTING CAMP — AM portable radio; CB radios, spotting scope with stand and/or auto-window clamp; extra tarps, sheet plastic, and poles (for covering hung game or gear stored outside); single-bit cruiser axe; chain saw with fuel and spare chain; chain oil; electric lantern; two-cell flashlight; fluorescent marking tape (to establish trail to downed game or whatever); meat saw; spare rope (brings lots); cots; sleeping bags; pack boards; day packs; folding camp table; folding camp chairs; cards and cribbage board; charcoal and starter fluid; toilet paper; large nails; folding toilet; shovel; paper toweling; fluorescent safety vests; first aid kit (see Chapter 15 for additions); maps; coat hangers (helpful for drying wet clothes); gas or LP lantern with fuel supply, plus spare mantles and generator; plastic garbage bags; insect repellent; wash basin with soap; monofilament tape (handy for many quick repairs including broken gunstocks); plastic bags for hearts and livers.

TENT CAMPING EXTRAS — Stove, stovepipe (with tent wall heat baffle); stovepipe wire; patching material (waterproof adhesive tape is a quick fix); seam sealant; spare tent pegs and line for extra tie-downs in storms; small broom for cleaning out tent.

COLD WEATHER GEAR — Snowshoes; snow shovel; paraffin fire starters; large broom for getting snow off tent roof or sweeping tent/camper entry free of snow; door mat for getting snow off soles before entering.

HOT WEATHER GEAR — Spare tarp for shade awning; Lister-type water cooling bag; extra camp coolers for spare ice supply; aerosol insecticide; fly-killing strips or paper; fly swatter.

COOKING GEAR — Stove and fuel; hot pad holder; griddle/fry pans; sauce pans; dutch oven; dishes; silverware; large cooking utensils (big spoons, forks, spatula); coffee pot; dish pan (metal, to allow heating water in it); dish rack (air drying is superior to wiping); dish cloth; scouring pad; detergent; water storage containers; wire whip for stirring pancake batter (these are easier to clean than are geared hand mixers); plastic wrap for covering opened foods; butcher/bread/paring knives; good can opener; decent sharpening stone.

SHOOTING GEAR — Rifles (include one spare per camp); lens tissue; cold-proof gun oil; cleaning rod; patches; appropriate cases and scabbards; targets and hearing protectors for any sighting-in shooting; minirangefinder (see why in Chapter 6); shooting glasses.

PERSONAL HUNTING GEAR — Binoculars (compact broadfields best for timber, 7 x 35 or 8 x 40 for general use); thermos, towel/washcloth; toilet kit, complete with shaving mirror and toothbrush; sunglasses; hunting knife; Chapstick; sun/windburn cream. How about spare eyeglasses if a pair gets lost or broken?

And don't forget the hunting licenses.

5

Guns and Glassware

Nothing activates dormant brain cells, oxygenates tired blood, and stimulates sluggish bowels more than arguments about what makes the ideal rifle and/or cartridge for mule deer. Selecting a rifle and cartridge for mule deer hunting admittedly is complex compared to arming for close-range, dense-cover whitetails on which a good hunter usually could make do with a 30–30 or 35 Remington. No reasonable man would say that of mule deer hunting. Even so, a lot of the Great Muley Rifle/ Cartridge Debate comes across like that of medieval theologians who argued about how many angels could dance on the head of a pin. Here's why.

First, cartridge power is not the key issue. Experts with strong theoretical ballistics knowledge and lots of hunting experience declare that when it comes to killing power, cartridge plus bullet count for about twenty percent, while marksmanship by the shooter counts as eighty percent. Or, it ain't what you got but how you use it, as the farmer's daughter told the garden hoe salesman.

Second, most muley cartridge arguments fail to address the prime question: Where and how is this Mr. Wonderful load and rifle going to be used? Mule deer hunting conditions vary a lot more than whitetail hunting. For several seasons, I once happily hunted cow-country muleys with a twelve-pound varmint rifle in the then-wildcat 25–06 caliber. Since heavy rifles are easy to shoot accurately, this beast was a deadly long-range combo. Yet it would be a miserable choice for fast handling in pinyon-juniper cover or black timber.

The sensible approach is to sort cartridge choices into three separate categories. That will do some automatic sort outs of rifle models; for instance, no pump or lever-action rifles for belted magnum cartridges. Any shooting outfit choice should be tied to the user's skill. If the shooter is mediocre with a medium-power rifle, he'll be much worse with a potent magnum. One complication is that in choosing a big-game rifle, many people hunting in the West logically have in mind both deer *and* elk.

Some cartridge performance figures are not precisely reliable. Ammo makers have a quaint habit of taking velocity readings with extra-long test-firing barrels whose higher velocities are then published with a straight face as gospel. Not running an independent ballistics lab, I can only quote factory load data *with* the reminder that normal-barreled hunting rifles often can't match those. Fortunately, the amount of variation we're talking about is not usually significant in the game field.

Discussed below are domestic cartridges with trajectories and bullet energy practical for two hundred-yard shooting, and bullet weights desirable for use on deer (varmint-bullet loads omitted). I picked two hundred yards as the maximum effective *hitting* range for many or most hunters. (Some of my guide friends call two hundred yards laughably optimistic and say one hundred yards is more realistic.) Shooting industry technicians say that 950–1000 foot-pounds of striking power at target (not at muzzle) is the minimum to reliably kill deer-sized game.

CLASS I MULE DEER CARTRIDGES – 1000 to 1600 foot-pounds of energy at two hundred yards. This includes the 250 Savage with a 100-grain bullet at a hair over 1000 foot-pounds of two hundred-yard energy; the 243 Winchester allegedly at 1400 foot-pounds with 100-grain bullets; the 6 mm Remington at about 1500 with 100 grains; and the grossly underloaded 257 Roberts for about 1080 foot-pounds with 100 grains.

Lacking power and suitable trajectory for reliable kills on mule deer at two hundred yards are such oldies as the 30–30 and its clones, the 35 Remington, the hotter 22 centerfires, the 44 Magnum, and some others that make respectable one hundred-yard deer rifles (the 22s do not). Skipped for obsolescence is the 30–40 Krag (30 U.S.), which roughly matches the 303 British still popular in Canada.

Published data for the 243 Winchester is clinically delirious even by the easy-virtue standards of manufacturer sources. In sporters, the 243 matches energy levels of the 250 Savage — both still good deer killers. The more hype-free 6 mm Remington is somewhat better. The 257 Roberts (nee Remington-Roberts), a cartridge with more lives than a cat, is easily hand loaded to significantly higher power than the anemic factory standards. (Thanks to today's confusion of the civil justice system with playing a lottery, I will not publish any hand loading data to set me up for a lawsuit.)

With 100-grain hand loads, my custom 257 over the years has produced more instant kills than any cartridge I've used, up to and including the 300 Winchester Magnum. Don't ask me why, because I don't know the answer. Nor can I explain why 117-grain spitzers in my 257 have never killed deer quite as quickly as the 100-grain spitzers. Perhaps 100-grain caliber bullets are some accidentally ideal combination of weight to mass to sectional density.

Also in Class I are the 7 x 57 mm Mauser 140 grain (1585 foot-pounds); the 300 Savage doing best with 150-grain loads (1400 foot-pounds); and the 303 British 180 grain (1500 foot-pounds). The U.S.-underloaded 8 mm Mauser belongs here. The 7 x 57, like the 257, does much better when hand loaded, and 150-grain bullets improve the 303 British deer performance.

Do not consider Class I muley cartridges only as wimp loads for kids or little old ladies in waffle stompers. Class I 24 and 25 calibers are accurate and reliable midrange deer killers. Recoil is typically 7 to 12 foot-pounds, or about half that of the 270 or 30–06. Some Class I's do well beyond two hundred yards in the hands of marksmen. Some also lend themselves to light, short-action rifles. Finally, 6 mm and 25 caliber cartridges make good varminters for off-season sport and great marksmanship training.

CLASS II CARTRIDGES — from 1600 to 2000 foot-pounds at two hundred yards, start with the 6.5 mm Remington Magnum 120 grain (officially rated at 1830 foot-pounds at two hundred yards but much less in the Remington 600 bolt-action carbines once chambered for this); the 25–06 120-grain; 240 Weatherby Magnum 100 grain; and 257 Weatherby Magnum 100 and 117 grain. These turn up about 1700 to 1900 foot-pounds at two hundred yards. Even so, 24 to 25 caliber bullets and the 6.5 120 grain are poor for heavy-boned wapiti.

Better choices for combination deer and elk hunts are the 1800-plus foot-pound two hundred-yard performance of the Norma-loaded 7 x 57 Mauser; the 7 mm –08; the famous 270 Winchester; the theoretically better 280 Remington; the sadly overlooked 284 Winchester; and the rimmed 307 Winchester. We also have here 308 Winchester and 30–06 cartridges too well known to need description. The neglected 358 Winchester and the rimmed 356 Winchester make the list as good muley and elk midrange medicine, particularly in timber's typical closer range.

With their greater power, Class II cartridges are more versatile big-game loads than in Class I ammo. But recoil ranges from about 14 to 24 foot-pounds. Along with high noise level, that can hamper once-yearly shooters and beginners. And *all* shooters get kicked crosseyed by Class II's upper range of cartridge power in featherweight sporters. For good rifle shots, most Class II rounds will take mule deer to three hundred yards or more. Those from 270 up will grass well-hit elk at least to two hundred yards. (Poorly hit elk are tough to anchor with anything not fired off wheels.) Factory ammo in 270, 308, and 30–06 is conveniently available everywhere in the West, including crossroads gas stations and Ma and Pa stores during hunting season.

In Class II, the 30–06, for all of its eighty years, makes most sense for a deer-elk combo. For deer only, the 270 gets the nod. The rival 280 is a better round but may wind up an orphan with adverse effects on ammo-buying convenience and rifle resale value. Many serious riflemen-hunters today are reloaders. It's difficult to buy empty 280 cases for reloading, and this reloading brass shortage, whatever the reason, may be why 280 caliber has been a sales counter blue baby since birth years ago.

CLASS III CARTRIDGES – over 2000 foot-pounds at two hundred yards, are for expert riflemen who can accurately shoot anything not requiring an artillery carriage. Included are the so called magnums, starting with the 264 Winchester 140 grain (2270 foot-pounds); any of the 7 mm Remington Magnum full-power loads (2210 to 2500 foot-pounds); a couple of blue ribbon – 06 loads (if factory data is believable); the excellent 300 Winchester Magnum's 2300 to 2800 energy; and the obsolescent 300 H&H Magnum. The Weatherby 270, 7 mm, and 300 Magnums all belong to Class III.

Above 30 caliber are the 350 Remington Magnum (just above 2000 foot-pounds); then come the similar-performing 8 mm Remington Magnum and 338 Winchester Magnum with from 2500 to almost 2700 foot-pounds at two hundred yards. Beyond is King Kong country, home of the 375 H&H Magnum, the dying 350 Norma Magnum, and the 340 Weatherby. It's safe to say that the Class III cartridges above 30 caliber are chosen primarily for elk or big, irritable bear, with muleys only as secondary targets – and heaven help the shooter with bursitis.

The lightest bullets in various calibers are to be avoided despite their oversexed trajectory data. They remain more wind-drift vulnerable and unnecessarily meat destructive. In the good old days of multiple deer tags, I took a 243 Winchester muley hunting with extremely accurate 85-grain varmint loads. These killed deer like dynamite, but whole shoulder quarters were pulped by these thin-jacketed, violently expanding bullets.

On the other extreme, my son last fall hit a running Montana muley buck through the chest cavity with a Weatherby 7 mm Magnum 175-grain Nosler—his favorite elk round. Due to limited bullet expansion, the deer made three hundred yards with no blood sign showing until close to where it died. Fortunately Pete's a good tracker and found it shortly. The moral here is that heavy bullets designed for bigger animals often don't expand reliably on deer.

Despite some whopper tales, most Rocky Mountain mule deer are comparable in size to northern whitetails. Even with 6 mm and 25 caliber, I've never lost one. The desert subspecies run a bit smaller. On animals this size, a heavier bullet's lower velocity and/or heavier jacketing adds up to less bullet expansion—which reduces chances for a quick kill. For example, in the popular 270 Winchester, a 130-grain load tends to kill deer quicker than 150-grain bullets. In the timeless 30–06, 150- to 165-grain bullets put deer on the ground faster than most 180-grain loads. But as the example of 85-grain loads in a 243 Winchester shows, light bullet choice can be overdone.

Where the wicket gets sticky is choosing a compromise bullet for lightly framed deer and elk that have a relatively massive skeletal structure. Too light a bullet may start breaking up when hitting large elk bone. The reduced bullet mass has less capability for deep penetration into heart, lungs, and aorta.

My rationale is that if there's a bullet performance failure, a wounded deer is much easier to recover than a wounded elk. For combined deer-elk hunts, my choice therefore is to choose ammo primarily with elk in mind—but *not* go overboard. Instead of, say a 175-grain bullet in a 7 mm magnum, I'd pick a 160-grain bullet. Ammo and bullet makers have made strides over the years toward the ideal of bullets that open up well on game, yet hold together for deep penetration. Nosler partition or solid-base bullets are one example.

In summary, the main factors in choosing a mule deer cartridge involve the hunter's shooting skill and tolerance of recoil, plus some common-sense consideration of how and where he plans to hunt. Once-yearly hunters are *not* skilled riflemen. The moral is either do enough off-season shooting to take stout recoil and muzzle blast in stride, or stick to Class I or one of the milder Class II cartridges. True, the more powerful loads have greater long-range potential. However, don't think that auto-

matically makes the shooter into a long-range expert. It can work per-
versely the other way. A guy who's a decent game shot with a 308 may
turn into a trigger-jerking flincher with a 300 Winchester Magnum.

*   *   *

In recent times, four long-established American gun makers have
gone out of business or are wheezing in the bankruptcy code's economic
oxygen tent. Thus, any commentary on specific rifle models risks being
obsolete before it sees print.

Mule deer hunting is basically bolt-action rifle country for two reasons,
one valid, the other pure pickle smoke. For muley hunters who want
magnum cartridges, slide and lever actions admittedly are no dice. The
other reason given for bolt-action predominance is "greater accuracy." On
paper, the average bolt action beats the average non-bolt repeater, but the
difference is really meaningless out where the hair and hide are.

The average non-bolt repeater today has more inherent accuracy that
the overwhelming majority of shooters can use. Typically, autoloaders,
lever, and slide-action rifles today will shoot three-inch groups at one
hundred yards. It takes a very good shooter to keep his shots in four- five-
inches with *any* rifle under field conditions. Therefore, if your rifle is
something like a Savage 99 or modern Remington slide action for a suitable cartridge from 243 Winchester to 30–06, you are definitely in business to take mule deer. In fact, for hunting muleys in black timber and the
high chaparral or low, you may be in business better than with a clumsier-
repeating bolt gun. The vital factor is not what kind of monkey-motion
makes the rifle work but how well the hunter *shoots* it. That includes
modern single shots available in Class I or II or III cartridges from 243 up
to 338 Winchester Magnum.

Today's bolt-action-rifle buyer — if he hurries to beat further manufacturer bankruptcies — never had it so good. He can buy anything from
a 6-pound synthetic-stocked ultralight, to more conventional 7½- to
8-pound sporters among the more than fifty makes in big-game calibers
on the American market in 1985–86.

Actually, the choices are even wider, since some suppliers have several models to choose from. Prices range from about three hundred dollars into several thousands. The majority of these rifles are foreign imports subject to abrupt disappearance (along with parts availability) as
importers drop product lines, get dropped themselves, or whatever.

Synthetic stocks are the only really new rifle wrinkle in many years,
and are far better than the short-lived Tenite plastic stocks on cheap
shotguns, circa 1940. Manufacturers avoid the pathetic practice of trying

to make today's plastic stocks look like wood. (Even at age 13 when I loved anything that burned gunpowder, I conceded that wood-imitative Tenite gun stocks had the esthetic charm of high-gloss cowflops.)

Today's plastics have the virtues of great strength and lightness. They make ultralight rifles possible (which are great to carry but difficult little demons to shoot accurately). Thanks to the compressibility of synthetics used, these space-age stocks also soak up some shoulder recoil, a nice bonus. They're not cheap, but neither is halfway decent American walnut, the standard gunstock material for well over a century.

One of the best features of the synthetic stock is that it won't swell or shrink with humidity changes, a common cause of rifles changing zero. Some gun gurus preach that barrels should be tightly bedded, with or without some mysterious shimmed pressure points determined by witch-

Bolt-action rifles, like Pete Nelson's Weatherby 7 mm Magnum, lend themselves to potent cartridges. Such a rifle is particularly useful when you're combination-hunting mule deer and elk.

craft and human sacrifice. Only a Druid would put that much faith in wood stability. A tree trunk is a giant wick so permeable that the tree sucks water two hundred-plus feet high through that "solid" wood. No wonder Forest Service researchers say wood cannot be truly water-proofed. Except in arid climates, a tightly bedded rifle cannot hold zero. Even if tight bedding shrunk groups an inch today, the wood swelling in tomorrow's rain will alter barrel pressure, possibly changing zero enough to miss game.

Therefore, a bolt-action rifle should: a) have its action tightly bedded in glass-reinforced epoxy (easy-to-use kits are available); and b) free-float the barrel, that is, enlarge the stock's barrel channel enough that the barrel is permanently clear of any swelling or shrinking of fore-end wood. Proper free-floating is a delicate job best farmed out to good gun shops.

In vogue today is the "classic" stock with no Monte Carlo cheek-piece. High-combed cheekpieces logically evolved for better scope-aiming stability. With scopes here to stay, the less-supportive low combs of most classic stocks are a subversion of common sense and good field marks-manship. Why then are gunmakers sticking us with these throwbacks to the era of iron sights and buggy whips? Because, omitting cheekpieces, they can use thinner stock blanks to fatten their profit margins. So, hoping that Barnum was right, they keep snowing us that classic stocks look nicer and restore lost manhood. If you just like to look at rifles, get a classic stocked rifle. But if all you want is to shoot better and faster with a scope, a cheekpiece aligns sighting eye and scope without rubbernecking. As a bonus, it reduces recoil to the face, a painful place to soak up recoil energy.

*   *   *

Just as the Model T was the car that put America on wheels decades ago, the Weaver K series scopes of the late 1940s put glassware on Ameri-can rifles. There were older scopes and better scopes, but the mass mar-keting of the rugged, low-cost Weaver K's was Revolution Number 1.

Revolution Number 2 was the arrival of variable scopes in the 1950s. While fixed power scopes freed American hunters from the shortcomings of iron sights, variables freed them from the shortcomings of fixed-power scopes. By then, many hunters knew that 2½X scopes, fine for timber, couldn't hack it on longer shots. I learned that early using a spare rifle with a 2½X Bear Cub. Confronted at two hundred yards with two jittery bucks who kept changing places, I couldn't tell with that low power which buck was which and wound up taking the lesser animal.

But sometimes a timber hunter needs extra magnification. I lost a

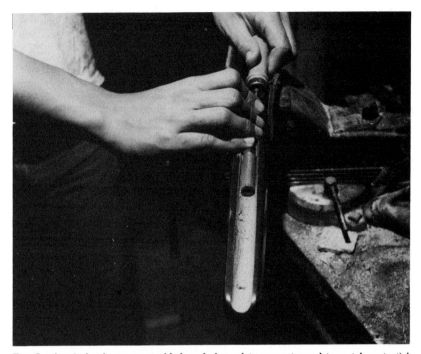

Free-floating (enlarging a gunstock's barrel channel to prevent wood-to-metal contact) is essential on bolt-action rifles to prevent shifts of zero with changes in humidity.

chance at what was likely a big buck at about ninety yards because it was walking head down, probably scent-trailing a doe. That kept his entire head screened by tall grass that my 3X Leupold lacked magnification to peek through. No antlers seen, no shot fired. There would have been time for the twist of a variable's magic ring to possibly save that day.

On the other hand, the thirty-foot field of a typical 4X scope then and now is too narrow for close-range timber hunting, as I also learned to my sorrow. In woods or brush, shots may be fifty yards or under. There, a 4X field shrunk to fifteen feet or less is inadequate to quickly locate partially concealed standing deer and hopeless to keep track of running game.

Since a mule deer hunter may work open country and thick timber the same day or even the same hour, a variable-power scope is ideal for him. By now, three types are standard: 1.5 to 5–6X, 2 to 7–8X, and 3 to 9X. For mixed timber-brush-open-country hunting, a 1.5 to 5 or 6X scope is excellent. Their low-power field of view is huge (up to seventy-plus feet). For hunters working primarily open country, variables in 2–7X are all that's needed. Oversized 3–9X scopes are ponderous on even medium sporters, let alone light rifles. Bear in mind that 9X has little field of view if the standing buck you intend to snipe suddenly starts running. Recent years have seen a trend to more compact scopes. Check specifications before choosing one. Reduction in scope size is accompanied by smaller fields of view, some of them too tight for timber hunting.

The option of higher magnification offers a little-known bonus called *twilight factor*. This rating of dim light performance is based on multiplying the unobstructed diameter of the objective (front lens) in millimeters by the magnification (4X or whatever). As it works with a typical 2–7X scope, the twilight factor at 2X is 7.75. At 7X, it's 14.5. You'll then see almost twice as well in poor light, such as a dark and stormy dawn.

Another caution. Variable scopes are complex optical instruments. Cheap ones involve cutting corners in design and materials that can and do lead to disastrous failures. One Montana outfitter told me he had so many clients whose low-priced scopes went bad that he now keeps spare rifles on hand for those unfortunates. But often they missed good mule deer and elk in discovering that their own scopes had packed up and quit.

Usually you get what you pay for. My earnest advice is to buy the best scope you *can't* afford! I'd rather buy a lower-priced rifle (within reason) and stick the extra money into more scope quality than go the route of an expensive rifle and a cheap, prone-to-fail scope, which is exactly the syndrome my Montana guide friend marveled over in so many clients.

Today's scope market contains about eighty big-game models, far too many to itemize, and changing often on an annual basis. My all-time favorite is the Leupold line, which is both optically and mechanically excellent, and priced accordingly. I've had scopes that were reliable for years in bitter (but dry) cold in the Rockies fog internally their first day of hunting in the mild but very wet coastal climate of the Northwest. But never has a Leupold fogged on me. I've also had excellent service out of Bushnell scopes.

Fixed-power scopes still have a place. Not as delicate as some variables, good ones can take hard service. They tend to be lighter and naturally are cheaper. In fixed power, 4X is the best choice. For occasional woods use, a couple of 4X models have more field than the usual thirty feet.

Rectangular lenses for wider field are good in theory. However, in practice, manufacturers have had big problems in hermetically sealing these. In one season, I had three Redfield 2–7X wide-field scopes fog on me — one of them new, another just back from a factory resealing job after earlier fogging.

Today's duplex crosshairs are fine for mule deer hunting either in forest or open country. A good dot is optional, but the post reticule has no place in longer shots.

The biggest problem with rifle sighting systems today is the commonly inadequate mounting systems. We're still stuck with fragile 6–48 scope-mount screws in most mounts. These became standard decades ago both when scopes were small and light and recoil factors were less (example: Winchester standard Model 70s that topped eight pounds). Today we take very light rifles often in more potent calibers, slap on variable scopes fifty percent heavier than fixed-power scopes twenty-five years ago, and expect the same dinky 6–48 screws — all pitiful four of them! — in the mount base to hold it all together. Also working against our tinhorn mounting systems is that we *use* rifles harder nowadays. Three decades ago, not many rifles were bounced around in 4wd rigs and all-terrain vehicles. Now it's common.

Nor are such Mickey Mouse base screws the only rat in the corncrib of rifle accuracy. Last fall I had trouble sighting in a light rifle in a 358 Winchester. Despite fully tightened screws in the rings, the scope tube slid with every shot due to inertia (a somewhat heavy scope plus light rifle equals plenty of recoil). That changed bullet impact eight to ten inches each time. I'd be more philosophical if that occurred with my 340 Weatherby's awesome recoil. But a 358/200-grain slightly tops 30–06 recoil, half that of big magnums. I "solved" the problem by applying Loc-Tite metal adhesive to the rings' interior surfaces.

Much effort by the shooting world has gone into achieving a higher degree of super accuracy by way of better big-game bullets and barrels. But even at longest range, we really don't need varmint rifle accuracy to hit deer chests that are seventeen times the target area of a crow or prairie dog. And of what use is our fixation with accurate barrels, ammo, and marksmanship when our scope-mounting technology remains so primitive that we end up relying on glue? Is the auto industry still using Ford Model A engine mounts?

Based on hard experience, the best advice I can offer a serious hunter is to mount a scope as follows: First, degrease all screws, base, and rings, with alcohol. Do the same with screw holes, using a twist of rag on a round toothpick. Similarly degrease scope tube and inner scope ring surfaces. Finally, mount the scope using Loc-Tite or a similar metal-thread adhesive, including the interior scope ring surfaces. Make sure you have screwdrivers that fit the small screw-head slots perfectly for maximum tightening.

In light of this problem, what's the best mount, you ask? First of all, forget the awkward see-through or tunnel mounts that manage to violate

Swing-over scope mounts like this one on a Savage 99 allow use of auxiliary iron sights without the too-high scope positioning of see-through mounts.

every design precept of good scope mounting — too high, too awkward to use with a scope, too vulnerable to damage. With normal mounts, the problem is not the mount per se as much as the too-small screws. Over the years, the best zero-holding mount I've ever used is the hinged, low-swing Pachmayr side mount. It allows iron sight use if the scope is snow-plugged or whatever. The design is flawless, and most important, it's mounted with much larger screws.

The long-established Redfield Jr. top mount and its imitators are good but woefully dependent on the tiny 6–48 mounting screws with their propensity to loosen in some forms of transportation (examples: light plane vibration, 4wd rough motoring, or saddle scabbard use). If you hunt hard, ask your gunsmith about redrilling and tapping your hunting rifle to use larger-mount screws. Even then, I strongly recommend Loc-Tite.

At best, scopes and mounts are rather fragile systems. If you want to lose your stomach lining quickly, put a bore sighting collimator in your rifle, mount the whole schmeer in a padded vise, look through the scope at a mark, and just push lightly on the scope tube with finger pressure. You'll see the crosshairs develop St. Vitus' dance. The surprising thing is not that we have scope problems. Rather, it's amazing we don't have a lot more.

In summary, if you have a rifle that makes inch groups at one hundred yards, wonderful! — even if it has no more relevancy to ninety-nine percent of big-game hunting than the color of your boot laces. But if your musket only makes two- to three-inch groups, don't morosely convert it into a stove poker. Not many years back, that was considered fine accuracy, and it's still all the accuracy needed to put meat on the table and antlers on the wall. Of far more practical importance is having a scope mounted as securely as you or your gunsmith can arrange and (in bolt guns) having a free-floated barrel that won't rezero itself the first day you hunt in rain or snow.

6

Marksmanship for
the Muley Hunter

"**W**hich is the biggest one?" Dave Petzal's voice was a half-octave higher than his usual monotone, proof that he was excited. It's the equivalent of a high scream in anyone else.

Through binoculars, I picked the best of two bucks alternately bounding and trotting, as Dave quickly dropped into a sitting position. It was well he might risk taking that time for a steadier shot. The deer were a good three hundred yards off.

Tough shot — fast-moving game at the distance of three football fields. Dave's 280 Remington roared. The bigger buck went down. I kidded Dave that that wasn't bad shooting for a decadenteasterner (pronounced as one word, like damyankee). Dave, as Executive Editor of *Field & Stream* magazine, is generally stuck in New York. But in the words of a poet, his heart's in the highlands. And it was superb shooting — a form of craftsmanship based on serious effort and *practice*.

No one is born a crack rifle shot any more than he or she is born an under-par golfer. That I know from teaching a lot of people basic marksmanship in the military, as a state firearms youth training instructor, and training my own family. Yet anyone of normal physical endowment can learn to shoot a rifle passably well.

What's amazing is how many hunters refuse any systematic learning of marksmanship. If taking up golf or tennis, they'd want some lessons or training, then would practice to acquire enough skill to make themselves happy. But when it comes to shooting a rifle, a lot of guys vaguely think that by some cultural-genetics magic they're deadeye descendants of Daniel Boone and Alvin York. Another hallucination is that buying a good rifle and scope makes the user a competent shooter.

This is a chapter on rifle shooting in mule deer hunting, not basic target marksmanship. However, target marksmanship is the basis for any real skill with a rifle. When you have to take a tough field shot in a hurry, you'd better be well enough grounded in fundamentals like trigger and breathing control that you don't consciously worry about them. *Then* your brain is free to concentrate on doping lead, range, wind drift. The fundamentals of rifle marksmanship can be had in many books on the subject (try your local bookstore or library) or in materials put out by the National Rifle Association, 1600 Rhode Island Avenue NW, Washington, DC 20036.

The best investment a serious rifle hunter can make is to buy an air rifle. This ends the excuse about "no place to shoot." A stack of old magazines will serve as a target backstop, and a living room's length is all the range you need if the target is small. Despite lack of recoil realism, an air rifle can teach fundamentals of breathing and trigger control that are as basic to marksmanship as learning the alphabet is to reading.

The positions to concentrate on are offhand, sitting, and the squat. The latter is not covered in shooting texts that I've seen. But it's faster to assume than sitting and steadier than offhand shooting, particularly in a strong wind that rocks the standing shooter.

None of us like offhand shooting if we can avoid it. Nonetheless, it's often shoot offhand or not at all. With practice, you may surprise yourself. Keep the left arm and elbow *under* the rifle, not stuck out to the side. Good trigger mastery is the key to decent offhand shooting.

Sitting can be done two ways. The standard mode is with feet akimbo and the elbows pushed into the hollows *inside* the knee joints, not on the rounded tops of the knees. The other mode is to sit with legs crossed for greater stability of the whole body. But the shooter hunched lower to rest elbows on thighs may face brush obstructions.

Prone shooting is steadiest but rarely practical. Even tall grass then blocks vision. Prone shooting is often okay from high ground at a target below. Another drawback of the prone shot is that you can't swing readily on a fast-moving target.

Skip the unsteady kneeling position. It lingers on in formal target

Open-country hunting for mule deer puts a premium on good field marksmanship, a coordinative skill developed only by practice.

shooting texts only as a century-old military throwback. The squat is just as fast to assume as kneeling and steadier in the bargain.

Admittedly useless in close timber, a steadying sling is the muley hunter's best friend on long shots. Of my nontimber deer kills, about half have been made with at least the helpful "hasty sling." In this, the left arm is put through the sling and the wrist is jammed into a tight half-wrap of the sling immediately below and behind the front sling swivel. Even steadier is the full military sling wherein two layers of forward sling are spread apart to allow insertion of the full arm instead of the quick wrap of the hasty sling.

This takes extra time. But when a full sling can be used, it's a truly great accuracy aid. Hunting in badlands, I once jumped a small herd of muleys very close. They zipped over a canyon edge so fast that I barely glimpsed a big set of antlers in the rush. I ran to the edge, but they had vanished in gullies below. Betting they'd appear again, I sat down quickly and slipped on the full military sling of my heavy 25–06. The herd came into view, and slowed to a trot directly away from me up the far side of the canyon. I put the crosshairs between the buck's antlers and a tad above, noting at the time how steady the sight picture was. Due to the risk of only wounding game, I dislike long "stunt shots" and trigger-happy hunters who habitually try these. But sometimes a shooter knows instinctively he will pull it off. The first bullet, squarely in the neck vertebrae, killed instantly. I counted 418 broken-ground paces to the buck — probably an honest 350 yards. Using the sling, the shot was easy. But without a sling, I'd never have tried it.

Hunters often overshoot game at steep uphill/downhill angles. That's because gravity drop has less effect on bullet flight at a sharp angle from horizontal. If you are shooting either up or down a forty-five degree slope at 300 yards game, bullet trajectory will behave as if range was a *horizontal* 210 yards (source: *NRA Firearms and Ammunition Fact Book.*) Correction can be calculated for different angles of steepness. But in hunting, there's rarely time for mental math even if you did know the slope angle. Which you won't without the experienced eyeball of a civil engineer.

Don't despair. My rule of thumb is to hold on the bottom line of a critter *steeply* above or below. With the bullet striking high, that results in a centered hit. In thirty years of hunting often in steep country, this nonmathematical crudity hasn't failed me.

Sighted in at lower elevation, does bullet point of impact change when fired in much higher country? Yes, but even at 10,000 feet, the change will be only a half-inch *high* at one hundred yards with spitzer bullets and no more than an inch high with round-nose slugs, according to NRA ballisticians. Thus with typical pointed-bullet ammo sighted in *at sea level*, you could be off no more than 1.5 inches on a three hundred yard shot at 10,000 feet. But most muley hunting is done well below that, and a higher altitude's change of zero can be largely ignored by the big-game hunter.

After a long rough trip in 4wd or on horseback, it may be a good idea to check where the rifle is shooting *if* this testing can be done where it won't spook game. This shouldn't take more than a couple of shots, unless zero has changed for some reason.

Many mule deer hunters worry themselves sick about range estimation. Truth is that *when rationally sighted in,* modern cartridges shoot trajectories flat enough to eliminate such worries over all but the longest ranges. The name of the game is to sight in for an optimum range at which (without any worrisome guesswork) you won't overshoot at mid-range trajectory *or* undershoot until way far yonder. But ignoring this great advantage, many hunters blindly cling to sighting in at one hundred yards. Their defense always is, "Oh, that's far enough. I've never shot a deer farther than that anyway."

Okay, let's check that out. Packing your faithful 30–06 with 180-grain deer/elk ammo, you see the buck of your dreams at — what — two hundred yards? Or is it three hundred? Here and now, do you know if you even need to hold high on him? If so, how much? You *don't* know?! Frankly, neither do I — not without looking it up. But I can tell you for sure that the buck won't stand there ten minutes while you do the arithmetic.

Your one hundred-yard sighting will print a 180-grain 30 spitzer between fourteen to fifteen inches low at three hundred yards. If you hold right on the centerline of his eighteen- to twenty-inch thickness top to bottom, you have nine to ten inches leeway, meaning you'll shoot five to six inches below the chest cavity. To center his engine room, you'll have to hold about five to six inches above his backline — *if* you can accurately eyeball how much that is out there at three hundred yards.

But let's say you do manage to hold five to six inches high and squeeze off a perfect shot from a convenient rest. Horrors! Turns out he was really only two hundred yards. Darned if you didn't shoot over him, since your one hundred-yard sighting gives just four inches of drop at two hundred yards.

Now let's say your rifle instead was properly sighted in for two hundred yards. Without further ado, you held for the center of his chest and let drive. Down he went, because if he was two hundred yards that's exactly where you hit him. Out to about 260 yards, you still put a bullet low in the chest (about seven to eight inches under centerline) to take out heart and/or ventral artery. At three hundred yards, you could miss the main chest cavity but still smash the lower shoulders. If low-hanging mountain mist fooled you, and he was only one hundred yards, the bullet should hit two inches high from the center of his chest. (This data is from modern ballistics tables but will vary somewhat with rifle-barrel length, ammo brand, and bullet shape.)

A golden rule on long shots is this. When in doubt, hold high on the chest but *not* above it. Rarely with today's flat trajectory cartridges do hunters undershoot. Instead they often miss by holding too high.

Range estimation by eyeball is an art. Most hunters overestimate distance, particularly on a successful shot. But sometimes it's easy to underestimate. Our minds judge distance by comparisons. Certain optical illusions can fool the brain badly. Distance is easily underestimated when looking across canyons, for example. Unable to visually evaluate the sunken ground between it and the distant point, the brain tends to ignore it — and thus underestimates.

Not surprisingly, we tend to estimate distance in timber country by unconscious mental reference to size of the prominent objects, which are trees. I grew up hunting in runty timber in northern Minnesota. When I began traipsing western forests with far bigger trees, I grossly underestimated distance at first. Once I blithely took a stand covering a canyon bottom I thought was 200 to 275 yards distant. When my driver-sons came through, they were tiny, and I realized slant range into the canyon bottom was a solid four hundred to five hundred yards, well beyond range of my 257.

Varying light conditions can fool the eye. Terrain features like hills seen under starlight or a dim moon look closer. To me, early dawn makes objects look farther. Very bright sunlight can make light-colored things appear closer. A deer silhouetted against the sky can appear much closer than it really is.

Inevitably, various range-finding gimmicks have appeared on the hunting market — game-framing wires in the scope, or a dot reticule of known size. Example: a dot that covers four inches at one hundred yards when almost covering the eighteen-inch-thick chest of a buck tells you that he's close to four hundred yards distant. In the past, I lapped up such stuff. But in practice, I've found they're not important, although a dot has the separate virtue of making a good aiming point on running shots. Again, with today's flat-shooting cartridges sighted in properly, range estimation out to 275 to 325 yards is rarely that critical. Few riflemen have any business shooting at game beyond, and even then there's the nagging ethical question of humane kills despite good hits.

The hand-held Rangematic is a miniature split-image rangefinder that I've tested to be accurate as claimed to plus or minus five percent out to some hundreds of yards. It's handy not to take a reading on flighty game but to premeasure questionable areas. My son and I once argued about whether a certain vantage point was feasible for shooting at any deer across an semi-open basin containing big timber. He thought the maximum was two hundred yards. Remembering how big trees have fooled me, I guessed 350 to 400. We were both wrong; the Rangematic said three hundred. This is more than academic. Previously, I mistakenly would have passed up a shot across the basin. He could have missed one due to underestimation.

Most shooters are vague about how much wind affects bullet flight. Wind drift of the bullet increases at a faster rate than range itself. For example, with a 270 Winchester 130-grain load, a 20-mph side wind moves the bullet only about 1.5 inches at one hundred yards. However, when range is doubled to two hundred yards, bullet deflection goes up fourfold to six-plus inch, which is something the shooter must reckon with.

At three hundred yards, bullet displacement of nearly fifteen inches is ten times greater than at one hundred yards. Since the West is often windy country, that's one reason why long shots are tricky. Mountains and canyon-scarred badlands can be full of unpredictably veering winds. If taking a long shot, try to notice from grass or foliage movements out near the target how much wind is blowing and from what direction. Bullet-flight physics are complicated, but take it on faith that in a given caliber, the reduced slow-down rate of a longer (which means heavier), more streamlined bullet makes it somewhat less vulnerable to wind drift, even though its muzzle velocity is lower than a lighter bullet.

Windy weather is also chancy shooting because of what strong wind can do to the shooter. In a near-gale, I once jumped a handsome buck at about ninety yards and had to fire quickly offhand. The wind buffeted both me and my light rifle so badly that the crosshairs gyrated all over the deer and landscape. I got him, but with a misplaced first hit in the rump that ruined both hams. If you have a choice, carry a heavier rifle in such weather. The real lightweights are harder to shoot accurately any time and much more so in strong wind.

*   *   *

In my first deer season, I learned three vital lessons about hitting game on the run. My forty-five hunting seasons since then have borne them out many times in shots of my own and by companions.

I heard Uncle Ralph fire a shot. When I got to his ridgetop stand, he was out in a spruce-muskeg swamp cleaning a big whitetail buck that I guessed was 130 yards from where Ralph fired. He snorted at my range figure and said it was no more than ninety yards. Accurate pacing wasn't possible in the snowy muskeg. But Ralph's estimate was probably close. He was a forester, and distance measurement is a tool of that profession. (The other best distance estimators are varmint hunters and surveyors. If you hunt with one of these, his range doping is worth listening to.)

I asked him how far he led the target. Ralph cheerfully said he had no idea but that it must have been enough! At the time, I didn't think I'd gotten much for my money in deer lore on my uncle's fine buck shot. Actually, I learned a lot.

The first lesson is that most hunters overestimate shooting range, just as I did in guessing how far out that buck had been from Ralph's ridge. Maybe we habitually overestimate as some instant-anxiety reflex.

Two, it's almost impossible for a shooter to explain how far he led the target. Here, the shooter probably tends to underestimate. He remembers some kind of sight picture when the shot went off. But to save his life, he usually can't tell more than that. His reflexes just outstripped his memory recording capability. Typically the shooter cannot swear whether he was spot shooting at a fixed point ahead of the game, or maintaining a constant lead ahead, *or* taking a very fast overhaul lead. The latter, often called the "paintbrush" by shotgunners, gives the illusion of shooting just a short distance ahead of a moving target. Actually, the lag of the shooter's eye-brain-trigger-finger coordination, plus trigger plus firing mechanism plus cartridge-ignition time means the fast-swinging gun muzzle and bullet moved a good deal farther ahead of the target than the gunner probably realizes.

The third lesson impressed on me by Ralph's deer kill may be the most significant of all: The best shot a hunter has on running game is often his first one. If the shooter knows his business, that usually does the trick.

Hitting moving targets with the aid of that marvelous scanner-computer known as eye and brain is an art, not a science. No memorized mathematical formula can tell you how much to shoot ahead when a buck bounds out of cover at a maximum rate of knots. There simply isn't time. Also, there are too many variables, particularly with an erratic, broken-field runner like the muley who is a tougher bounding target than the running whitetail. Just the hunter's reaction time is a major variable. That may be very fast at 8:30 A.M., but much slower late in the day, thanks to fatigue or even relaxed boredom just before the oatmeal hit the fan.

At that moment of truth, pure reflex action based on previous moving-target shooting is the only alternative to blind luck. Wingshooting experience with a shotgun is valuable to the rifle-wielding hunter. It also helps if earlier target shooting programmed the basics of sight picture (simple with a scope) and trigger squeeze into your mental computer.

On one ranch that takes mule deer hunters, the rancher's wife films the hunt with a video camera for a unique playback that night to the hunting guests. The video reveals that most misses are due to shooting too high. This doesn't surprise me, since my own mule deer misses are usually overshooting. I can best hit a bounding muley when it comes down, not when it's soaring well up in the air. As the buck lands on earth, he is stationary for a fraction of a second, cocking his legs for the next bound. The trick is to try to pick where he's coming down next and arrange to have a bullet there simultaneously. While not easy, it's still better than trying to hit an airborne muley who offers two lead problems—lateral *and* vertical. The best mule deer practice shooting is hunting jackrabbits with a rifle, because the jack is a similar steeplechaser.

A muley's bounding gait doesn't cover ground as fast as a spooked whitetail's run. Once, a game warden and I speedometer-clocked whitetails running scared on flat, no-obstacles terrain at 38 mph. While I haven't had the same chance to clearly time mule deer, my guess is that they don't go much over 30 mph. On broken ground it might be closer to 25 mph.

But even 25 mph is not loafing—it's thirty-seven feet per second. A muley doing that at three hundred yards will travel about twelve feet just in the approximately one-third-of-a-second time of flight for a fast-stepping 270 130-grain bullet. Now add the delay for shooter reaction and firing lock time. Then you understand why a hunter grossly underestimates his actual lead when he hits a long-range deer running at a ninety-degree right angle to him and claims to have only shot "just ahead of his nose" or "about a full [deer body] length ahead." A good twenty feet might be more like it for the "some-spot-ahead" school of leading game. Closer range shots or those quartering away naturally are easier than a ninety-degree deflection shot.

Just remember that your best shooting opportunity is likely your first one. If you miss that shot, you'll join the buck in a high-adrenalin panic. That helps him but may hinder you.

*   *   *

Assuming a normal hunting cartridge, good shot placement is vital to prevent wounded or lost game. Many sportsmen believe the best hit is through the chest cavity behind the shoulder, or that a neck shot is even better when it can be made.

I flatly disagree, both from personal experience and because of the medically expert opinion of my chief hunting partner. An ardent big game hunter, he's an M.D. specializing in emergency medicine, runs the emergency room of a hospital in a sizable city, and did internship and residency in a bigger city's main hospital that provided plenty of gunshot cases. (Bear in mind that the physical makeup of man and deer are very similar, although deer seem to be less shock-susceptible than equivalent-size humans.) Here are the good doctor's views on shot placement:

• The neck shot is unreliable on deer. Only a small area is occupied by the spine and the two carotid (jugular) arteries. A hit in the neck that misses those may only stun the animal, which might recover and escape. The neck is also a small target subject to quick, erratic movement anytime the deer moves its head. (I almost lost a buck that was neck-shot very close with a 284 that missed spine and arteries.)

• A brain shot kills but makes a sordid mess of a trophy's head. Too often, a shot aimed at the head hits the animal in nose or jaw, which may permit escape and later death from starvation.

• *A suitable bullet in the shoulder area is the most reliable way to both immobilize and quickly kill any North American big game.* First, the shoulder area is a large target. Second, a hit almost anywhere there does lethal damage. Unlike the neck shot, precision is not needed. A low bullet breaks the upper leg and continues into the heart. Hitting higher, the bullet has a good chance to sever the aorta, the main "freeway" of the circulatory system. This often drops the animal faster than a heart shot — perhaps due to quicker blood pressure collapse. (Heart-shot deer often make a furious run for a surprising distance, then die — often out of sight and hard to find.) Placed higher yet, the shoulder shot destroys the scapula (shoulder blade) and may fatally sever the spinal column. Between spine and brisket, a typical big-game bullet, already expanded by passage through the upper leg bone or scapula, does maximum lung damage, partly from bone/cartilage splinters as secondary missiles.

• Second best is the classic behind-shoulder shot. Unless the shot is at a sharp angle, it's likely to miss both heart and far shoulder. A bullet passing between ribs to enter the lung cavity sometimes doesn't expand properly. In any event, death from the behind-shoulder shot may not occur for some time. Meanwhile the animal may have full leg mobility to run at top speed into escape cover or out of sight. Another drawback of the behind-shoulder shot is the chance of making an inhumane, disastrous hit in the closely adjoining paunch instead.

The doctor-sportsman makes sense. Many hunters object to some loss of meat from a shoulder shot. But would you rather lose a few pounds of low-grade shoulder roast or the entire animal from a less disabling hit elsewhere? Even if not killed outright, a deer with one or both shoulders broken is usually knocked off its feet if standing, and invariably if running. In the unlikely event it regains its feet, it cannot move fast or far with broken shoulders unless helped by a steep downgrade.

Some hunters don't regard a going-away shot in the game's rear as a reliable one. My experience has been that most modern cartridge/bullet combinations will penetrate far enough to reach the vital cardiopulmonary area up front. Such deer are a mess to clean, of course.

Never regard a shot as a miss because the animal vanished or kept going with no sign of a hit. Somehow mark or remember from terrain objects where the deer was when shot at. An immediate compass bearing can be useful. Then, before leaving your spot, mark it by hanging your cap or handkerchief on brush or a tree limb. That's a vital reference point when you get out to where you think the animal was at the shot. Try to find its tracks. On sun-baked soil, that may be impossible. Snow is a different story. Look hard for hair. Almost always some is cut off by a bullet.

Blood sign says much. Bright blood with fine froth tells of a lung shot. If centered in the tracks, it probably means the animal is hemorrhaging from mouth or nose and isn't likely to travel far. Darker blood with green browse material shows a stomach wound, and fecal matter, an intestinal hit. Dark blood clean of debris can be either from the liver or right side of the heart (the left produces much brighter blood). Since the liver is located high in the gut cavity, its blood doesn't escape readily. A major liver wound is fatal, and the animal should be followed diligently. A lot of darker blood may well mean a right-side heart wound. The heart is located very low in the frontal chest and readily exudes blood. Except downhill, a heart-shot deer rarely travels more than one hundred yards. Medium-red blood without air bubbles may be from a nonserious flesh wound, but a lot of it indicates major arterial bleeding, which can be fatal.

If you can track the animal, pay attention to line of travel. A serious leg or shoulder wound will show stumbling or misplaced tracks. If not pursued at once, a wounded animal usually beds, first making a fishhook turn to watch its back trail. Each wounded game situation must be played by ear, but here are some general tips:

• If hours of daylight remain without other hunters around and signs indicate a chest or solid paunch hit, it's usually a good idea not to trail immediately. The animal will almost surely bed down if hard hit and unpursued. You can then trail within close range. But if snow, rain, darkness, or competing hunters are a threat, follow fast.

• When tracking, watch carefully to the sides as much as ahead for the animal suddenly getting up to run. Tracking here is best done by two hunters, one working out the trail, the other doing nothing but scanning intently for the animal.

• When blood sign is infrequent and hard to follow, two-man tracking helps. One hunter stays at the last-known sign while the other moves ahead looking for more. That way, you don't lose the original trail if you make a false move or two. When tracking alone, leave a bit of toilet paper at the last blood sign before scouting for more.

Tracking hard-hit game is difficult but usually not hopeless if you pay attention to detail and use common sense.

• A distant companion may clearly hear your bullet impact on game. Believe it or not, anatomical location can often be accurately guessed from the sound. A drumlike *plok* often means a chest cavity hit. A paunch shot makes an unmistakably water-sounding *pa-LUMP* noise.

No one wants to wound or lose game. The hunter has an absolute responsibility to try to locate an animal either wounded, or downed and dead. Since prevention always beats cure, good shooting at common-sense ranges means those problems will rarely happen.

7

Cow Country Mule Deer

As the throttled-back Cessna lost altitude, the heat-hazy landscape below became sharper, like bringing a lens into focus. "Wyoming," they named it long ago, which means "upon the great plain" in an Indian tongue.

The name is appropriate. This vast, seemingly empty land from our altitude looked like a tawny tarpaulin, only slightly wrinkled. That applies to much of the Great Plains west of the Missouri River.

My amigo, Pat McFall, looked moodily below. "Where the heck is this great deer country you've been yakking about?" he asked accusatorily. "Nothing down there but a million miles of jackrabbit gymnasium."

This was back in the 1950s. Pat and I both lived in our native Minnesota then where he was chief warden pilot for the game department. We borrowed my father's plane to fly to Wyoming for Pat's first mule deer hunt. I'd already hunted there several seasons. As I too once felt, Pat was perplexed that this "great deer country" didn't have any forest. Where we'd grown up, in the north country, deer (whitetails, of course) live in plenty of cover. No timber or brush, no deer.

I grinned and told him, "The deer are there. Lots of them. Wait and see." And early next morning, I was teasing him for taking only a three-pointer at daybreak. He refused to be abashed. "Pure self-defense," he said, "he and about eighty other muleys were gonna run right over me if I didn't shoot." That was only a mild exaggeration.

The semi-arid Great Plains occupy a wide hunk of North America from western Canada down into Texas and Mexico. Even more arid farther south, the land is desert rather than shortgrass range. The separate Great Basin west of the Rockies receives much less moisture and doesn't hold as many deer outside of its adjoining foothills and mountains. Another vast plains habitat, the so-called sagebrush steppe province extends from central Wyoming across the Rockies into eastern Oregon, Washington, part of California, and as far south as Colorado. It has decent mule deer herds in some places, much lower numbers in others. Eastern Oregon, for example, has had trouble maintaining worthwhile numbers of mule deer in recent years. Eastern Washington hasn't done much better.

Although many of the bigger muley heads come from timbered parts of the West, where bucks have a better chance to live longer, Cow Country America can offer excellent hunting. The biggest-racked mule deer buck I ever saw was in such "jackrabbit gym" plains. At first startled look, I thought it was a stray elk. Paradoxically, plains mule deer hunting can be easy or very difficult. More on this later.

High deer populations in a lot of the West's open country are a fairly modern development. By the end of the 1800s, mulies were wiped out in some areas and were scarce for fifty years. Even within living memory, they weren't common during their slow comeback. My longtime rancher friend Dean Hall relates that when he was a youngster, seeing a deer was so unusual that he'd tell other kids at the little country school (to which he daily rode four miles on horseback in all weather). By the 1950s, sighting fifty to eighty deer a day was not unusual.

Why the scarcity of deer followed by plentitude? The answer involves a combination of factors. Starting with the first homesteaders after the Civil War, a rural population lacking refrigeration regarded deer as meat conveniently kept fresh until the rifle went off. My theory is that the coming of the Rural Electrification Administration (REA), starting in the 1930s, greatly reduced the overshooting of deer for food. REA made it possible for rural folks to buy or home-slaughter beef (the only real eatin' meat, says any cattleman) and keep it several days. Or indefinitely, once the home freezer boom hit after World War II. When you live fifty miles from the grocery store, don't think that isn't a revolution in lifestyle.

Meanwhile, Great Plains human populations declined in the lean 1920s and 1930s. That too reduced the meat-hunting drain on the mule

The largely treeless Great Plains hold plenty of mule deer. This seemingly open country offers deer the choice of a surprising amount of concealment.

deer resource. The eventual end of the Depression years' hard times maybe helped, too. One rancher told me, "No, can't say I like to eat venison at all. Back in the thirties, things were so tough that we couldn't afford to eat our own beef. We ate deer. To this day, venison only reminds me of hard times I'd rather forget."

Stepped-up coyote control demanded by sheep ranchers was far more effective when new poisons and aerial hunting arrived. One ranch I know of lacked coyotes for more than a decade. That sharply increases fawn survival and has been documented in many studies. Increased livestock watering impoundments on many ranges let mule deer establish locally where they'd never been before, particularly on parched uplands. More irrigated farming of alfalfa, nourishing feed that deer can't resist, probably played a role. These habitat changes can affect hunting tactics themselves, as we'll see.

The combination of sparse cover and plenty of deer of course spells fairly easy hunting for run-of-the-mill muleys. However, the bigger mule deer bucks in the Great Plains can tax the skill of any hunter. Cow country muleys can be highly nocturnal. I've seen seasons where none of our party scored on anything unusually big in the way of bucks. The real hat racks didn't seem to exist. But a late night trip on a rural road would reveal one monster buck after another in the headlights.

What were these big old muleys doing on the hoot owl shift? Going to feed in lowland meadows and alfalfa. However, they go long after dark and leave such vulnerable open areas well before daybreak. Let the lesser bucks, does, and fawns risk their necks trailing out of the purple hills before sundown or back when dawn paints long shadows in the sage. The old bucks are hypercautious.

How and where do you then find the bigger bucks in legal dawn-to-sunset hunting hours? Ah, that's where both the hard work and fun begin.

The fascinating thing about rangeland deer hunting is not the sheer number of deer in some places. Rather, it's how ingeniously the most worthwhile deer—the big bucks—use such relatively naked country to almost totally disappear. Much is rightfully said about how well whitetails can hide. But in typical whitetail cover, a large truck would be pretty well concealed if you could get one in there. The boss muleys of the Great Plains are the better magicians in my book, since they can vanish where you'd think nothing bigger than a jackrabbit could hide successfully.

Several scientifically observed factors about mule deer behavior are worth remembering by the hunter any time, and all the better in hunting open-country muleys. These are:

• Mule deer are animals of open country rather than timber, which means they are very good at taking care of themselves in country without much cover. *Don't underestimate their evasiveness even in seemingly bare country.* For one thing, that open country has more hiding places than you think.

• Muleys prefer distance rather than cover for safety. Yet they can do a good job of hiding when they wish. Muleys often choose to stay in open view of a predator if they have enough safe distance. But if the enemy disappears, the deer may promptly depart to travel far without stopping or hide themselves to watch for the suspected danger. This has been documented in scientific literature, and for what it's worth, I've noted such behavior often in many years of hunting or just observing mule deer.

• Muleys are basically herd animals. Bunching together is in itself an antipredator defense. Thus, a group of mulies often are casual about revealing themselves. By contrast—and this is tactically important to the hunter—where mule deer exist in limited numbers, they are far more secretive, and much less prone to hang around in full view. Why? Because deer, singly or in small numbers, are more vulnerable to predators—and they seem to know this after eons of dodging fang and claw. If a mountain lion successfully pitches into a herd of twenty mule deer, individual deer survival odds are a favorable twenty to one. (Well, not quite—the odds are much poorer for a rearmost deer and much better for the out-of-reach deer up front.) But when a lion makes a successful attack on a pair of deer, the odds are a dismal fifty-fifty, and of course are zero for any lone deer in reach of the predator.

With that in mind, remember that a big mule deer buck tends to be solitary a good part of the fall until the rut nears. With only his own senses to depend upon, a lone buck must be extra cautious. This vulnerability may be a reason for pre-rut bucks buddying up by pairs or sometimes in small herds.

• Since a lot of mule deer range is not Fat City in terms of available food, the animals must make up for it by having bigger "home" ranges. Naturally, that can pose a deer-locating problem for the hunter. Furthermore, scientific observers have noted that muleys are notably unpredictable about where and when they show up. By contrast, whitetails frequently are time-clock habitual. The mule deer approach to daily life is often (which doesn't mean always) here today, not here tomorrow. This in itself is an antipredator strategy, no doubt evolved over time.

• Finally, the high-bounding gait of mule deer, not really fast on level ground, is almost impossible for four-legged predators to match going up rough, steep grades. A scared muley therefore almost always heads for high ground, and the rougher the ground, the better. It has been calculated that the energy demand running uphill is twelve times greater than on level ground. The muley has the heart and lungs for this, its enemies (golden eagles excepted) do not.

The tactical moral here is that rarely will you find plains country mule deer any great distance from some kind of broken ground, the steeper the better. It need not be high, just so long as it's rough and steep. In lieu of actual hills, steeply eroded gullies and canyons will do.

*   *   *

Against that background or some of it, let me tell about one that got away, not once, but several times in open country with two fairly experienced hunters after him. The tale tells much about smart plains muley behavior.

The giant, elklike muley mentioned earlier is the classic example that sticks in my mind. In the early 1970s, Don Hendrickson and I were hunting a Great Plains ranch for deer and pronghorn antelope. The best antelope area was a couple square miles of gently rolling sage and grassland cut up by dry gullies six to ten feet deep. This area rarely held deer. Looking for pronghorns, Don and I split up and approached these plains from opposite directions. I saw a few small bands of pronghorn does and

Dave Petzal shot this six-year-old muley buck during an October hunt in Campbell County, Wyoming. The buck weighed 210 pounds and had a nearly perfect set of antlers.

fawns, then spotted Don waving hard and walking fast. When we met, he was excited. A monster buck deer headed my way, and hadn't I seen him?

That I hadn't, despite the nakedness of the country. No doubt the buck after fleeing Don at long range had hidden in one of the narrow, steep-sided draws. A big problem was no wind (rare on the Great Plains, but it does happen). That meant the buck was free to travel any direction.

I made a long backtracking circle behind a low ridge, then carefully hunkered atop it through concealing sage. From here I had a view of perhaps a square mile. Through my 8X binoculars I saw far-off Don sweep wide, then start methodically working along the edges of some of the gullies. Then my hair almost raised the hat off my head. About 150 yards behind Don, the grandfather of all muleys magically popped out of a draw, then bounded away in the opposite direction over a low hill. I stood up, yelled and waved my arms to get Don's attention when that buck was still in range behind him. Intent on those draws, Don never looked my way or heard me. Nor did he ever look behind him, which is a common hunter error responsible for many a muley buck dying of old age.

Don was less than charmed to hear my story when we linked up. "You should have shot in the air to get my attention," he grumbled. But at the time I feared the sound of even a distant shot might spook that buck right off the ranch. "At least I've got a good idea where he went," I told Don. I knew the area and quickly laid out a plan. That involved a squeeze play in which we'd approach a short but deeper gully system from opposite sides.

Those other draws were the only hiding place in the area where the buck had been heading. If he was still on the ranch, he'd be in there. When jumped, he might flee from one hunter and run into range of the other. Or we could get very lucky and bushwhack him at close range when he was still trying to play peekaboo in a gully-bottom's greasewood. I've done that at times, once shooting a high-crowned four-pointer at thirty yards rather to the amazement of both the buck and me.

I was right. The deer was in the gully complex. Unfortunately he did not play by the rules. Rather than curl up deeply within a draw and set himself up for a fatal ambush, the buck apparently stayed on his feet and kept watch over the edge, no doubt screened by sage or greasewood. Muleys can see and recognize hunters on foot at several hundred yards, and this one sure didn't need a cataract operation.

Don and I each started in about five hundred yards on opposite sides of the gully complex. Very quickly the buck—same old boy with the ridiculously big rack—came up out of the draws and lit a shuck. Furthermore, he knew darned well that he had two hunter problems at six o'clock and twelve o'clock. Naturally he bounded out toward three o'clock before we had a chance to close our five-hundred-yard distance more than a few paces. I watched him keep going half a mile to the line fence and on to another ranch where even binocs didn't reveal him any more.

We returned before next dawn in hope he might be back in the antelope sections. As I told Don, previous lack of hunting there may have convinced the buck that it was a good place to while away the October days before rutting season. Since he hadn't been smoked up by any shooting, I didn't think we'd scared him enough to abandon it, even if terrain and cover were not typical mule deer hideout stuff.

Again I was right. And again the buck gave us the slip—not once but three times. He likely night-grazed an alfalfa meadow not far away and then worked back into the pronghorn area long before dawn—probably before we arrived. Although we parked the truck half a mile away, he certainly heard the vehicle crunching ranch road crushed shale despite deliberately slow driving (and no headlights). There was enough moonlight for Don and me to hike separately to different places to squat in the sage and wait for dim dawn, then start wearing out our binoculars. But with a deer's night vision, Super Buck might have seen us coming. Soon I saw a flicker of gray movement far off. I barely managed to glass a glimpse of him, head and marvelous rack held unusually low as he slunk through thick greasewood, again well out of rifle range. Then he vanished about where I knew there was another draw.

Whether or not he saw us to begin with, he still knew we were there somewhere. He hadn't sneaked like that the day before when he had us pinpointed. I pulled a very cautious stalk of the area where he'd vanished. When close enough to start getting dry-mouthed with excitement, I happened to look to one side and saw him at better than a quarter mile, a distance he seemed hooked on. He was up on a low ridge, tolerantly watching me stalk the area he'd left half an hour earlier. When I stopped to glass him, he walked over the ridge and out of sight. I hoped to hear the distant thud of Don's 308, but he was nowhere near.

The buck fooled us a couple more times before we quit to take some consolation-prize bucks in the hills before our time ran out. That buck must have been a ballistics expert, because about five hundred yards was the deadline he always maintained. Regardless of what you may have been told, that's almost impossible deer-hitting range even with today's hot magnums.

Short of using an 81 mm mortar, how could we have hock-hung this antlered Einstein? The buck obviously felt he could handle us in his skimpy-cover terrain. He used those little gullies like a World War I trench system for concealment, yet did not blindly hide in them. He still kept posted on what we were up to. When uncertain where we were at daybreak on Day 2, he didn't stay in the draws to get ambushed but pulled a neat sneak to high ground from which to spot us. Sure, the buck had some luck that Don didn't turn around that first day and nail him the one time the deer was even in rifle range. The deer was also lucky that lack of wind both days didn't have him traveling in a direction we could predict.

In hindsight, we should have done these things:

1. Kept a sharp eye open behind frequently, since concealed big muley bucks are notorious for sneaking off when the unaware hunter has passed.

2. Maybe we should have parked the truck much farther off before daybreak on Day 2. Or possibly we should have made a quiet, fireless spike camp in that area to be there ahead of his predawn arrival. Anytime you have the game moving into a zone you're already occupying, chances of fried liver for supper multiply.

3. In trying a pincers movement on his second gully hideout that day, we both should have carefully stalked the area. Or alternatively, one guy move openly while the other remained out of sight in hopes that the deer

would unwittingly move toward the hidden hunter. As it was, the buck spotted both upright walking hunters.

That was my first experience with a big buck who forgoes hilly hiding places and opts for more open country, relying on distance more than concealment for his security. Such bucks can be very hard to locate. In one case, a team of five wildlife researchers using a radio direction finder repeatedly failed in basically open country to find a muley buck wearing a signal transmitter *and* a blaze orange collar! Using draws, small brush clumps, and tall grass, the deer made itself invisible and was iron-nerved enough to let the searchers pass within a few yards at times.

If even a radio telltale and a blaze orange collar don't give away a muley really determined to stay hidden, obviously there is no magic formula for hunting normal deer. It helps if the hunter first knows the country. A lot of range lands are laced with eroded gullies, and these are the typical hideouts for resident deer after sunup. Unless containing obvious trees sticking up, such draws are often invisible from a distance. To hunt them may require walking the very edges. Usually the gullies contain plenty of shrubs and grass. In their lower elevations, they often contain patches of hardwoods such as green ash or oak. Any of this furnishes good cover for deer holding tight as a pheasant. Rock ledges and washouts are added hiding places.

When hunting along the edge of such draws, walk very slowly with lots of pauses. That may flush a muley who might otherwise stay hidden. Working wider draws is best done with two hunters, one on each side. For hunting bigger draws, a third hunter is useful to work down through the ravine itself, kicking out brush or timber patches. Deer in those may stay hidden even during a barrage of rocks. Once I lobbed half a dozen rocks down into a wild-plum thicket only about twenty feet in diameter. Nothing happened. When my son, who was coming up the sizable draw, got within mere feet of the thicket, out spurted not one but three muleys, one a fairly good buck that we let pass.

All that is for close-holding deer. But some big grassland bucks don't hold that tightly. From bankside brush or shallow draws they may take off some hundreds of yards ahead of an approaching hunter. Here the best bet is a two-hunter team. One works along the draw. The other is maybe two hundred to three hundred yards ahead. He should be out of sight of any deer in the draw and well to the upwind side.

Upwind? Yes, that's a calculated risk. If a spooky buck bails out because of the actual draw hunter, it will hit the flat ground heading upwind. It is to be hoped that it won't have gotten the unseen flank hunter's scent earlier while the deer was down in the draw out of the wind. The trick is for the flank man to see that deer and nail it before it wheels and gets away elsewhere after either scenting or seeing him. Obviously the flank hunter better be alert, since he may have only a brief chance.

A hunter-wise deer in open range usually has more than one card to play. Once I thought I had a big gully-dweller pretty well pegged. Details aren't important here, but I worked a still hunt on his favorite gulch in which to escape upwind he stood a good chance of getting shot. Would you believe he bailed out *downwind* and bounded through a nearby herd of cattle? Of course I couldn't fire. Probably that was an example of the safety-in-numbers herd instinct on the deer's part rather than of genius-level thinking by him.

A lot of Great Plains muley hunting is in hill country. This varies all over the map—figuratively and literally. Much of the "plains" are corrugated with ridges, complexes of buttes, or minimountains. In other areas, the hills are really sides of canyons or wider valleys, with tablelands on top. Any hill areas are attractive to muleys for reasons already cited. Some elevations grow evergreen timber, usually pine. North slopes often have juniper, scattered or thick enough to qualify as timber hunting. Hunting plains deer in hill country naturally can be harder work for the hunter. Even if the elevations aren't mountainous, climbing a few hundred feet of steep banks and shale talus is a workout, particularly in the hot weather common in the West's autumn. Hunting such open hill country is often tactically simpler than locating or stalking smart bucks in the flatter grassland/sage country. You can use the broken terrain for concealment, and possible deer locations are easier to predict.

It's much like mountain hunting (see Chapter 9) but on a smaller scale and with much less forest cover. The rules are not complex but are still important. First, take the high ground, preferably before daylight. Second, do far more looking than walking. Third, stay out of sight yourself—avoid skylines. Fourth, pay close attention to such classic muley hill hideouts as heads of draws or canyons, rock formations, or brush and timber offering concealment. (And remember that a muley needs very little vegetation to hide in). Fifth, work upwind or at least crosswind, not downwind.

Weather conditions influence deer in such country much as they do elsewhere. In hot weather, look primarily in areas offering shade. This need not be timber. Even a shallow ravine offers shade if the sides are steep enough, all the more on north slopes. Deer in windy weather get in the lee of ridgetops or anything else offering screening, particularly when it's cold. On chilly days, plan to work south slopes. After rain or wet snowfall, deer often come out of bad-weather cover to better dry out— their hair loses some insulative quality when wet.

Much of the Great Plains hill country lacks water seasonally except when man-provided. As a rule of thumb, the Rocky Mountain mule deer subspecies needs water except when snow is available. (That may not be absolute in all areas. One study in Colorado showed that local mulies, lacking free water, seemed to make it just on vegetation moisture like the true desert mule deer subspecies does.) Generally, deer stay within a couple miles of a water source. How often and how much water they use depends on weather and what kind of food they're eating.

Wouldn't it be easy to simply ambush them at water sources such as stock ponds or tanks? Not necessarily. Under much hunting pressure, muleys seem to wait until cover of darkness before watering. Again, that's not an unvarying rule. Years ago, my partner Jim McFall counted over a dozen sizable bucks at a remote stock tank at midday in hot weather. However, that area was getting very little hunting disturbance.

Hunting the cow country may lack the built-in splendor of mountain hunting. But you can get captivated by the awesome sweep of the Great Plains. It has its own special beauty, particularly at dawn and sunset when the buttes and hills change color by the minute. I know of a table-land that juts partly into a wide valley. I'm not the first hunter up there. On this high, flat ground are perfect circles of football-size rocks, put there to hold down tepee edges in the wind. It was a good place for an Indian camp from which to watch for the dark forms of buffalo in the distant miles of grass-rich flats below. I always park there awhile to admire the view. I like to think that the lean, copper-skinned hunters whose tepee rocks remain enjoyed it too.

8

Hunting Mule Deer in Timber and Brush

In spite of the scenery in those John Wayne movies, the inland West is not all desert, sagebrush range, or Monument Valley. It contains vast amounts of timber and brushlands often used by mule deer. Because of the precipitation needs of forests, most western timber country is hilly or mountainous. Big evergreens (black timber) include different firs, spruces, pine, and western larch. Large areas are of smaller pinyon-juniper evergreens, others in aspen, oak, chaparral brush, or desert vegetation. Bottomlands often have cottonwoods and brush and increasingly have been taken over by western whitetails.

Most standing timber provides little food for deer. But any of it can serve as cover for deer at times. The muley hunter should know what those times are. Bad weather is one. For example, mule deer use dense evergreens during snowstorms. Wind chill there is reduced. Even in calm, cold weather, much less ground heat loss occurs, thanks to overhead cover. Mature timber also intercepts a lot of falling snow, so forest floor snow depth is a fraction of that in open country. In hot weather, timber or brush provide needed shade for deer, particularly in the arid, burning Southwest.

Deer also use timber and brush to evade predators, and man is one of these. Predation defense for deer starts with going where the predators are not. The truth is that many mule deer hunters dislike timber and brush hunting. Their relative absence compared to open country hunting pressure is not lost on the cautious, mature bucks. Therefore, the time to hit the woods for muleys is a matter of common sense judgment. When more open areas are being heavily hammered by hunters, timber or brush is often the best place to find big bucks. That is true of muleys in general if weather is unusually hot, windy, cold, or wet due to falling snow or rain.

So much for the whys of hitting the timber or brush to find muleys. Now for the hows. Basically there are four fair-chase ways to *locate* deer. Those are:

1. Staying put while waiting for game to come to you.

2. Still hunting, which is covering ground to find game whose location is not known beforehand.

3. Staging drives — programmed human disturbance — to move game toward fellow hunters waiting in ambush.

4. Trailing or following tracks of the quarry to locate and take it.

All four systems have their place at times in hunting brush and timber. Those appropriate times are often dictated by factors beyond control of hunters. Weather is one of those factors. So is time of day. The amount of hunting pressure in the area is still another.

The following is perhaps the most important statement in this book: *The mistake many of us make all too often in hunting deer is to arbitrarily choose our deer-locating method while disregarding the realities of weather and other factors.* Instead, we should thoughtfully match the hunting mode to the circumstances facing us. Those circumstances will be described along with each of the four systems already cited.

The stay-put system is more popularly known as stump sitting or trail watching (a term more appropriate for the hunting of whitetail deer than trail-disdaining muleys). It works best under these circumstances:

1. Where there's a high deer population. If deer are few, you can waste too much time in one place waiting for a suitable animal to show up.

2. Even with plenty of deer on hand, you must know the area well enough to pick a good spot from which to watch. As we saw in Chapter 1, mule deer have large home territories and are not very predictable about their routine movements.

3. There must be reason for the deer to be moving. When (for whatever reason) they're not moving, trail watching is a lost cause. The best times for trail watching are when deer are traveling from feeding to

bedding areas or vice versa, or because of direct human disturbance, rutting activity, or weather change.

4. When and where the trail watcher has at least enough visibility to match his effective shooting range. It can be difficult to locate a spot like that in denser cover, particularly in somewhat flat terrain. Also, the weather must cooperate. On one hunt, I took pains to reach a vantage knob within a mature, somewhat open forest of big ponderosa pine and Douglas fir. For the first twenty minutes, the view was great. Then low-hanging clouds moved in on my mountainside, cutting visibility from 250 yards to maybe 25. End of that stump-sitting hunt.

5. When the trail watcher cannot be scented, seen or heard by deer before they come into good shooting range. A common mistake by deer standers and trail watchers is to reach their position by walking through the area in which they hope deer will travel. This contaminates the key area with long-lingering human scent that often will stop deer and turn them back or into a long detour. This is not a theoretical problem. I blush to admit that I've thoughtlessly made this scent-contamination boo-boo many times. In open-country trail watching, the scent-alarmed deer may still be visible and in decent shooting range. But that is often not the case in timber or brush hunting.

For the trail watcher to be at least partially concealed is all the more important in the Age of Blaze Orange. Naturally, the hunter must be quiet, too.

Stump sitting is almost worthless in poor weather, such as rain or snowstorm, or in hot weather. The hunter is tempted to find a halfway sheltered spot out of the elements, then sit and wait for deer to show up. Guess what: the deer also are holed up in whatever shelter is appropriate for the unpleasant conditions. They won't voluntarily leave it. Exceptions are when they're kicked out by other human disturbance, or during the rut, or when weather-induced migrations are underway (see Chapter 10).

Windy weather is another poor time for trail watching in brush or timber. When deer can neither hear nor scent well due to strong winds, they dislike moving around unless forced to. More dependent than white-tails on eyesight, mule deer aren't quite as prone to stay put on windy days, but they usually won't move as freely as at other times.

*   *   *

However, such deer-anchoring weather is ideal for the still hunter. First, some definitions to avoid confusion. Still hunting is not stalking (see Chapter 12). The still hunter moves to seek game whose location he doesn't know in advance. He *hopes* there's game in the area he's hunting.

The stalker *knows* where the quarry is (or was, at least) and makes an approach based on that knowledge. That's why stalking is not included in the four cited methods of locating deer.

Still hunting is normally thought of as being done by a hunter on foot. However, riding a horse to look for deer is a form of still hunting — and a good one, too, since deer often fail to recognize a human rider on a horse, and further, horses are very quick to detect game (see Chapter 13). Even road hunting with a vehicle is a form of still hunting, though admittedly not as interesting as still-hunting on foot, but done a great deal nonetheless.

Here we'll stick to classic on-foot still hunting. The hunter must concentrate on three things. The first is to carefully pick his route for minimum noise and best tactical positioning. Example: Stick to high ground if practical, since he can see better from there. Second, he should keep his eyes open for any tip-off data, such as fresh tracks and droppings. While still hunting is not pure track trailing, the still hunter always has the option of doing just that if opportunity arises.

But above all, he must do his utter best to locate game before it senses him. In this contest, "first sighting" often decides who wins — hunter or deer. Of course, the still hunter is best off working upwind to prevent game from scenting him.

Constant alertness is the key to still hunting. First sighting often decides who wins — hunter or buck. *Jackie Nelson Photo*

No hunter can do all three things simultaneously. You can't watch for distant game and still keep an eye on your footing to avoid making noise. Therefore, do only one thing at a time. Move one or two steps to ground you have already eyeballed for obstructions or noisy twigs. Then stop, look, and listen—a lot. In timber still hunting, that's much more important than simply covering as much ground as possible. If you hit a good vista such as a canyon overlook, linger awhile to study it all the better. Look not just for deer but for parts of deer. Muleys use cover far better than many hunters realize.

Freeze if you hear a twig crack or other possible game noise. Still hunting opportunities include game that may be on the move in your direction. If you're not moving at the time, you hold all the face cards.

Highly effective is a combination of still hunting and occasional, short-term stump sitting. If you find a good vantage spot, stay there awhile. Once, I'd been leaning against a tree a few minutes when a muley buck suddenly leaped up from behind a nearby fir windfall off to one side. Probably he intended to stay hidden while I passed by. But my long pause freaked him out. This is not a rare occurrence in forest hunting.

Still hunting is easiest in more open forests, such as ponderosa pine or Douglas fir. In those, visibility usually is fair, depending on the age of the timber and how much low-level brush there is. Thicker stands of lodgepole pine have almost no brush but offer so many tree trunks that you can't see a great distance. Lodgepoles are also noisy forests for walking, thanks to the great litter of self-pruned branches on the ground.

Quaking aspen stands (nicknamed "quakies") are excellent cover for mule deer and may offer some feeding. But aspen is a short-lived species, and quakies often have a lot of dead, noisy debris to step over. Pinyon-juniper forests offer very limited visibility. That's also true of the more dense stands of alpine firs and spruces up near timberline elevations. On the other hand, these thick-foliage, squatty trees provide plenty of cover for the hunter. The trick here is very slow, quiet movement from one tree to another for maximum concealment.

The extremely dense vegetation in some desert areas is tough to still-hunt. The above basic rules apply here too: move slowly, quietly, and spend far more time looking. Two upland cover types in the southern Rockies and the Southwest that defy successful still hunting are thick stands of scrub oak and the widespread chaparral types. Your best bet in those is to stage drives.

Certain conditions assist the still hunter. One is a little breeze to help muffle noise. Strong winds are not so good. Wind-deafened deer are jittery, won't relax, and park where they can see well. They also then spend a lot of time on their feet. That makes them easier to spot. But standing, they're in a better position to spot the ominous flicker of your movement at a distance in the timber. Also favorable are leaves and grass damp enough to make less swish and crunch noise. Rain helps mask small noises that even a careful hunter makes at times. Snow consistency varies greatly. New wet snow can be too squeaky to still-hunt unless wind is strong enough to cover the noise. Fallen snow undergoes a natural change of crystal structure in time that makes it quieter. But this may take a day or two. Crusted snow is hopeless for quiet walking. That's no great loss, since deer shun any crusted snow area if they have an alternative.

Obviously the still hunter must avoid personal noises — coughing, rustling candy wrappers, clinking a gun barrel against brush. Soft wool garments are best for this work. Alternative: old laundry-limp denim — the softer the better. Also desirable is a soft cap with enough bill to help shadow your face in the dim forestscape. Except in very open cover, a hat can be too noisy for still-hunting. Lug-sole boots are not good for pussy-footing. One trick is to slip old wool socks over them. Better, have softer-soled footwear in your daypack that you switch to before starting a serious, blood-in-your-eye prowl of the timber for that thirty-five-inch buck you just *know* is in there — somewhere.

Hunting from horseback is actually a form of still hunting, all the more because a horse can move very quietly in this much soft snow — and is far better than a human at detecting game.

* * *

When it comes to staging drives as a mule deer hunting tactic, there's good news, and there's bad news. First, the good news. Drives can be a very useful tactic to kick hidden mule deer out of cover. Although mule deer adapt readily to hiding in cover, they are prone to take off when disturbed. For safety, they tend to rely on sheer distance rather than close-range evasion like that superskulker, the whitetail.

Now for the bad news. Just because the mule deer is more easily driven than the whitetail does *not* mean that drives are a surefire method of meat-poling a nice muley. There's many a slip between the drive and the skinning knife here. Flight by driver-disturbed mule deer doesn't automatically mean a dash into the open for instant spotting and easier shooting by the standers. Many western forests and brushlands are simply too big for that. They may comprise entire sections or even townships of almost unbroken timber. (To give you some size perspective, a section of land is one square mile and contains 640 acres. A township in land measurement is six miles by six miles, or thirty-six square miles, which is 23,040 acres.)

Furthermore, muleys simply do not stick to specific trails as do whitetails. The muley's evolutionary heritage programs these open-country deer for escape in any promising direction when threatened. The whitetail developed in forests and swamps where getaways from predators were and still are fastest on established trails. Therefore, it is much harder to forecast precisely where a driven mule deer will travel. The more open nature of many western forests usually allows deer to flee without following trails.

Back to the good news! Don't give up hope of making successful mule deer drives in big timber. First of all, muleys are more likely to use the fringe zones of such big forests. They're really not true forest dwellers. Don't worry about how to drive muleys in the center of a sizable forest, since they are not too likely to be there. All you really have to think about is how to stage deer-moving drives somewhere in the fringes of a really large forest. How much fringe zone? That varies with terrain, type of forest, amount of hunting pressure, and so on. My observation over the years has been that a belt not more than a quarter-mile into the timber is where most mule deer sign occurs. Farther into the timber, much less sign. Don't take that as gospel. If there is a very good knob a mile back in that timber, a local big buck probably knows about it and may well be holed up there. Another factor that sometimes leads to deeper penetration of a given forest by mulies is water availability. But generally, mule deer in timber are not far from some edge environment.

Such edge zones are not just around the outer perimeter of the forest but also apply to timbered or brush areas surrounding any substantial openings *within* the forest. These include natural openings or manmade clearings such as logging clearcuts or power line rights of way.

The basics of driving deer are:

1. Do not try to push deer downwind. Sometimes it can be done with muleys in open terrain. But to chase deer in cover in a direction where their scent defense is useless is asking them to play Russian roulette, and they know it. Sometimes a badly startled deer may dash a short distance downwind but will very quickly turn upwind in order to scent any danger ahead.

2. Not surprisingly, standers directly upwind in the deer's line of travel will be scented and avoided. There are some exceptions. One, the scent of a stander on high ground might be wafted too high (particularly on a warm day) for deer to detect it. Two, from some limited experience, I think that a powerful dose of skunk scent placed in the stander's area can mask his human scent. More on that in Chapter 12. But as a rule, standers must be *well off to one side* of the anticipated escape route. The stander still needs a reasonable shooting view of the driven deer. Finding a stand with both attributes can be a neat tactical problem. Usually the stander is best off on some elevation, a hill, outcrop, or even a stump.

3. In total absence of breeze, staging drives is complicated by the fact that driven deer then may go *any* direction. With muleys, the likeliest bet is uphill — the stock reaction of mule deer to danger.

4. Nothing ruins a drive's chances faster than deer being tipped off about the impending ambush because they hear or see the stander. Remember too that they are not color blind. When wearing blaze orange, the stander needs some good concealment, which can be another tactical complication along with the "wind gauge" and a good field of view and fire. Who said deer drives in timber are a cinch?

5. A stander can also spoil a drive if, reaching his post, he walks through and thus scent-contaminates the area the deer are expected to enter to offer him a shot. This was already explained in the section on stump sitting. Remedy: Approach your stand from a rear side or whatever, just so you're not stinking up the same ground you're hoping deer will cover.

6. Usually any close human disturbance will move a group of muleys typically led by a paranoid dominant doe. But big old mule deer bucks are almost as cagey as whitetails in lying doggo while a nearby hunter goes past. The litmus test here is whether the concealed buck can keep track of the hunter by hearing and/or sight. The deer starts unraveling if the human stops for a while where the buck can't see him and now

can't hear him, either. If the animal worries enough, it will leave cover, either sneaking or making a dash for it. Therefore, the most effective way to move mature bucks is a slow, quiet drive with plenty of ominous pauses by the driver to rattle the nerves of any nearby hidden buck.

7. Be realistic about your available manpower versus the size of an area you plan to drive. Biting off too big a chunk is futile if there aren't enough drivers to comb the place reasonably well or enough standers to cover the likely escape routes.

8. Drives work best when: a) the involved hunters (or at least the drivers) know the terrain; and b) when they function well as a team. Some chaps are just too free spirited for this. This is the type who soon gets bored assigned to a stand, then takes off to do his own thing. Or unilaterally changes location so that his hard-working drivers push deer through an area where no shooter awaits. I don't know of any hunter who's been shot for leaving his stand before the drive came through. But I know the thought has crossed some drivers' minds. Mine, for one.

Staging deer drives is a complex way to hunt. But two or more hunters using some common sense and (it is to be hoped) knowledge of the area can get deer this way when other methods won't work. Sometimes muleys aren't moving for the stump sitter due to weather or midday lull. Sometimes still hunting is down the tube due to too-thick cover or noisy walking conditions (example: squeaky new snow). Then good drives may be the only game in town. And a highly interesting game at that.

*   *   *

The fourth deer-locating method is trailing. Usually this is a late-season hunting system for mulies. Trailing is rarely practical in mule deer country before snow flies. Tracks are too hard to find and follow on the dry, sun-baked soil.

An obvious exception is after rain. But here is a serious drawback. Autumnal rains in the West can be downpours. After those, anything that moves leaves tracks except on rock. However, much of the West has clay soils that become like glue when wet. Walking is then out of the question due to a massive buildup of highly adhesive mud on the soles of any footwear. Except from horseback, hunter mobility is crippled, ironically at a time when nonsnow tracking could be done in some terrain. You virtually cannot walk more than one hundred paces without spending several minutes scraping a few pounds of mud off your boots.

Some mule deer seasons (Wyoming, for one) open and close too early to take advantage of tracking snow except in high elevations. But not always. Premature snowstorms can hit in early October. (Homeward bound from a Wyoming muley hunt in the first week of October 1985, I had to break trail on I-90 after midnight in my pickup truck through eight to ten inches of Montana snow for 110 miles. That storm should have provided some dandy hunting in northeastern Wyoming where the season was open.)

During a snowstorm well ahead of the November rut, the buck is likely to be moving to some shelter he has in mind, traveling upwind, of course. If the tracks start to meander here and there, keep your sharpest eye open. That means the deer was looking for a bedding spot. In fact, even now he may be watching you. Where is he? Put your binoculars on brush, small evergreens, heads of draws, or rock outcrops that offer windbreak shelter.

Mature muley bucks, like whitetails, have an ingrained survival trick. They'll often make a sharp fishhook turn, then bed downwind of their trail. Thus they can scent any predator following their tracks. So look *very* sharply downwind when you find the tracks starting to wander left and right. In fact, stop and spend several minutes looking if you're in timber.

I learned that far back in my muley-hunting years when I trailed past a rimrock outcrop overlooking a juniper-studded draw. I was too bemused by the current aimlessness of the previously straight big-buck trail in the early fresh snow. A rock's clatter made me spin around just in time to see a white rump framed in big antlers vault out of sight. Running to the knob, I saw him beyond the juniper scrub, half a mile distant, and still carrying the Denver mail for all he was worth. At first I hoped this was a different buck. Picking up the trail again educated me. Yes, that Pony Express was my buck. He'd made a loop to that outcrop, let me walk by, then vamoosed. Simple trick, simple hunter.

That brings up a major difference between mature muley and whitetail bucks. Rarely will a spooked whitetail in typical whitetail cover run right out of the landscape like that. Instead he'll stop soon, circle, and hide to watch his backtrail. A disturbed muley may not stop for three miles or more. If the tracks you're following show a break into a run upwind, it means you're not likely to catch up to that deer this day. Not unless you have hours of daylight plus miles of ambition in your legs.

When in November a buck's brain turns to biology, the trailing game is affected. His wandering is to look for does. At this time, too, the tracks of a whole herd of muleys are worth studying closely for signs of a big set of buck prints. Look to the sides of the herd's trail, since a buck often travels a short distance from his does. The best thing about buck trailing in the rut is that you're dealing with a deer who has effectually lost a lot of his marbles. Do your best to avoid spooking any does with a buck you're after. If they take off, he's gone too. If they stay, he is very likely to remain or not go far.

In deeper, soft snow, tracks are not easy to read. First, make sure you're not backtracking the wrong direction. A deer's foot projects forward. Even if you can't see the bottom print, ascertain the forward angle of the track's penetration, then go thataway. Of course, sizing a hoofprint is harder in fluffy snow. Pay attention to the span between left and right tracks. Big bucks make a substantially wider trail than do the narrower does.

Another clue to the sex of a deer you're tracking is any urine sign. Deer urination in a circular mode probably means a doe. An elongated pattern is typical of a buck. Alas, deer inconsiderately may go long distances without urinating, particularly in chilly weather when they're not taking much moisture.

Estimating the age of a track is important — is it fresh or old? Yet aging tracks is very imprecise. Too much depends on the temperature and moisture content of the snow and what air temperature has been doing. Autumn snows are usually (not always) wet. A substantial snowstorm is often followed by a sharp temperature drop. That quickly firms up a track in the wet snow. Unfortunately, this means it shows little sign of its actual age and can still look reasonably fresh (less than an hour) when it is actually several hours old. Examine these quick-frozen tracks very closely. Look for bits of fresh snow that fell into them, any snow blown in by wind, or determine how much weed seed or evergreen-needle detritus has landed in them. If clean, they're probably anywhere from an hour to a half-day old. Frost crystals in them probably mean they were made during the night.

Often an early snow is a light one followed by a warming trend. This is easier for the tracker. Rising air temperature quickly deteriorates the sharpness of tracks. If the air temperature is above freezing and the track still looks sharp, you've got a deer perhaps only minutes ahead.

On a virgin snowscape, deer tracks can be seen a long distance on a hillside or terrain below you. With sharp 7X binoculars, you can then pick out tracks up to about half a mile distant if the sky is overcast. If the sun comes out, you might be able to glass tracks a mile off, since their indentation shadows will show up. A very useful trick here is to wear deep yellow or orange sunglasses. These darken anything blue, and blue is the color of shadows in tracks on snow. This heightened contrast makes tracks stand out remarkably in the distance. But blue sunglasses, which are an abomination, have the opposite effect.

Naturally, great alertness and lots of looking ahead and to the sides is a must in trailing game. If terrain and light let you do it, try to follow the tracks off to the side a bit. This is a defense against the deer pulling that same fishhook backtrail maneuver described a few pages ago. If you see the tracks ahead starting to meander, then making a turn, very likely that's what the buck is doing. At least you're forewarned and can play your cards accordingly, depending on terrain.

After getting faked out by that long-ago backtrail buck, I took the lesson to heart. About four years later I had occasion to hit the high ridges and scattered timber in fresh snow and soon picked up a large, apparently fresh track, going upwind, of course. I deliberately left it and made a wide half circle, moving fast because of the extra ground I had to cover. The return leg brought me back to his trail well ahead of where I'd left it. Again I pulled a wide half-circle maneuver. When I cut back, using as much concealment as terrain allowed, there was no sign of the deer trail.

That meant I was ahead of him, because he'd stopped somewhere. Hoping he hadn't already picked up my scent, I cut back off to the same side I'd just been on and then worked a slow, cautious stalk of the place I picked for a likely buck bed—a rocky knoll with a few scrawny young pines on it. That was a very bad place to try to stalk him, because I'd have to approach him uphill. But there was another, taller knob off to one side of the wind direction. Always maneuvering to both use cover and keep my scent from blowing into the target area, I got to the bigger knoll about 250 yards from the one I reasoned he might be on.

Still, I was stumped. Ten minutes of binocular study didn't reveal even an antler tip. But then what Kipling called the red gods of hunting gave me a break. The cold wind began picking up sharply. I put on a spare down vest from my daypack, hunkered down and decided to give it an hour's wait. In only half that time, like a magician's trick a standing buck suddenly materialized on the rocky knob. Either he planned to leave for more windproof shelter elsewhere or was just up to relieve himself before lying down out of sight again. I didn't wait to find out and picked him off. He was only an average-sized three-pointer. But the work, excitement, and payoff of some hard-learned trailing tactics makes that deer spell "trophy" in my memory, far ahead of several better bucks taken much more easily.

9

Mountain Muleys

As my son and I sneaked up to a rocky knob to peek into the huge canyon network below, we split up to study different areas. Peering around an alpine fir, I saw nothing more than a distant eagle soaring below. In an early season, we were hunting the east-facing ranges of the Cascades. To the west is Columbia blacktail deer country, to the east, Rocky Mountain muley range. In this alpine overlap, the deer are often hybrids—long black tails but "real muley" racks.

Peter gave a pursed-lips rabbit squeak, our close range come-hither signal. Backing away from the canyon rim, I hunkered over to his vantage point. My eyes caught two white spots on the far canyon wall. "Ah, goats," I murmured, although we were hunting bucks, not billies.

"Heck with the goats," Peter muttered. "See the deer couple hundred feet higher?"

I mused that we were hunting mule deer *above* mountain goat summer range, which is high country indeed. Glassing some more for deer, I smiled, thinking of an eastern friend who told me that mule deer hunting was overrated. No, he hadn't done any, but he figured that it would be a cinch in "all that wide-open western terrain." If I wanted some *real* deer hunting, he continued, I should go with him after whitetails in the dense timber and swamps of Michigan's Upper Peninsula where swamps are wet, forests are jungles, and men are men. Well, I've hunted close to half a century of whitetail seasons in the kind of northern forests of the Lake States that he referred to. And that can be tactically difficult hunting. But I also know that in such country, one hundred feet rates as a high ridge. Pete and I at present were close to a mile above sea level. Hunting farther south in Utah or Colorado, we'd be even higher. From the road's end trailhead, we'd climbed a good 2,000 feet on our hind legs. That in itself was some hours of very strenuous work.

Actually there are different types of mountains and hill country in the West's mule deer range: foothills, middle elevations, and the sub-alpine timberline stratum. Some of this country can be classed as arid, some of it is well watered. The differences of elevation, terrain, and rainfall mean wide variations in types of habitat. So much is written about lower-elevation muley hunting that many sportsmen fail to realize just what great mountaineers these hill-country deer are. Mule deer can handle the steep, rocky crags, the thinner air, the often turbulent and occasionally violent weather. The hunter who pursues them had better be prepared for the same challenging environment. Mountain hunting is hard work much of the time and hairy some of the time. But going after mountain muleys is *always* a great hunt, the kind you remember years after you've forgotten many less-demanding lowland hunts.

Also, higher elevation is probably the best bet for real trophy bucks today. In country easier for hunter access and much less difficult to hunt, bucks have far less chance of living the several years it takes to reach trophy size. But in the last decade or two, the irruption of 4wd and all-terrain vehicles has resulted in more hunters in the mountains. Inevitably this has tended to have two results. First, heavier hunting pressure whittles down the number of really big bucks in some areas. Second, once the season opens, the explosion of hunter disturbance soon forces deer to change their routine and start spending more time avoiding hunters — less daylight feeding, bedding in less accessible areas. Mule deer quickly learn to shift a few hundred feet above the ends of any vehicle roads.

In theory, mountains do offer some advantages to the hunter. Sometimes it's easier to both spot and shoot deer there than in flatland forests that offer no elevation advantages to the hunter. Furthermore, mountain country often restricts or funnels deer travel. Example: a canyon flanked by no-access cliffs. Not much imagination is needed to realize that deer going up or down there will be confined to that canyon.

The best basic tactic for hunting mountain mule deer is to get above them. Like bighorns and goats, mountain deer spend more time worrying

Getting high enough in mountain country offers the tactical advantage of being above the deer for easier spotting. Also, the activity of hunters at lower elevations often pushes deer up to the high-country hunter.

about threats from below than from above. Mountain winds are often too strong or fluky for reliable scenting and also limit deer's hearing. So they must rely more on their eyesight. The hunter who is adept at using terrain to stay out of sight while managing to really eyeball it himself has a lot going for him. Often that means extra walking or climbing in order to take advantage of the best cover. A firm rule here is to stay off the skyline. Forget everything you ever heard or read about deer having poor eyesight. Mule deer, as already cited, have excellent vision.

Use your own eyes *all* the time, preferably with the help of the best binoculars you can lay hands on. Normal human vision is at least as good as a deer's and is far better with binoculars. As one guide colorfully put it, "Lots of real hard looking in mountain hunting is like sweet talking a wealthy widow. You can't hardly overdo it."

Knowing where to look for deer is important. Unlike elk who prefer hillside benches big enough for a whole herd to bed, muleys often bed on relatively steep slopes. From there they can see below very well as a rule. In warm weather, they want shade. In chilly weather, they like some

Binoculars are almost always a part of mule-deer hunting, and especially in mountain country.

windbreak shelter, be it brush, timber, or rock formations. When it's downright cold, they avoid north slopes and stick to south-facing ones for sun warmth. If there's no sun, they'll tend to bed in dense evergreens, which have a warmer microclimate.

Far and away the easiest time to spot mule deer is when they're on the move. Usually that's early and late in the day. Two major exceptions to this are the rut and in migrations. When deer are moving, stay-put hunting is effective if you know from experience or just common sense where deer are likely to be traveling. Although muleys are rarely as trailbound as dense-cover whitetails, they tend to use certain routes at least until their routine is broken by too much hunter disturbance. Such routes may have several randomly used alternative trails.

In one hunt, I knew that a canyon cutting through some of eastern Washington's black basalt cliffs was used by higher-elevation deer to reach a lower basin offering feed. The kingsized coulee was too wide to cover from just one side. It actually contained half a dozen deer trails wending through the sagebrush. No one trail seemed to be the main commuter route. I had to cover the whole canyon. A thirty-foot-tall lava "haystack," relic of some ancient eruption, stood almost in the middle. Although not a rock climber, I got up there in late afternoon. The perch was uncomfortable, but the command of about 250 yards of canyon on either side was excellent. In the last few minutes of legal shooting time, I was rewarded by a medium buck trailing some does as they moved down-canyon toward an alfalfa field. However, this was on the opening day of hunting season. After enough hunter disturbance in the next day or two, deer might have quit using this ambush-vulnerable route until after dark.

Even with more hunting in the mountains than ever before, high-country muleys in my experience may be likelier to feed and water in daylight hours than are more heavily pursued foothill and lowland deer. For one thing, mountain deer must work harder for a living. Often there is less available food in their rugged, possibly arid or semi-arid home. They have to spend more time going to it, finding it, and eating it as compared to lowland deer who can stuff themselves in short order after dark in a flat, easily accessible alfalfa meadow.

Drinking water can be important to most mule deer. Generally, the uplands of the West get more annual moisture than adjoining lowlands. However, the hand of man through irrigation, stock ponds, and surface water management gimmicks has put a lot of water into what originally were very arid lowlands. A lot of the less-watered country today is in lower- or middle-elevation hill regions where seasonal moisture runs off quickly and not much man-supplied water is provided. Snow's arrival frees muleys of their dependency on surface water.

As a general rule, look for mountain muleys feeding in canyon bottoms, basins, or draws where seasonal water runoff means better soil moisture. That usually means a greater variety and better quality of plant foods. Given the chance, deer are gourmets, too.

One of the best places to find deer in timbered country is where logging, fires, or land clearing for range manipulation have occurred. Mature forests provide cover but little food for deer. Whenever old trees are removed, new plant growth develops, which usually benefits deer. In steep, timbered country high enough to get heavy snow, avalanche chutes are good feeding areas. Recurring snowslides keep bigger timber growth cleaned out of these chutes. Smaller brush — often good browse species — is supple enough to be flattened by avalanches without being destroyed, although sometimes pruned severely.

Usually, brush in avalanche chutes grows badly bent over from the tremendous snowslide punishment. Deer usually can negotiate such witch-tangles. But often the brush is so thick that a man has to get on his hands and knees. So the best way to hunt brushy avalanche tracks is to cover one from a nearby vantage point, preferably one you can reach quietly before daybreak, watching for deer feeding there. Flatter terrain at the foot of a chute where an avalanche runs out also offers good feed due to the extra soil moisture left by all that snowmelt.

Important to hill- and mountain-country hunting tactics are air currents. The first rule to remember is that air rises as the morning sun turns on the heat. This means an upward thermal drift that can carry your scent to deer above. On cold days, that uphill air flow is much less and can be overwhelmed by cold wind blowing over higher ground and running downhill. Late in the day, air flow reverses. Higher elevation's cooling air starts flowing downhill and again wafts your scent with it. That late-day downward flow in places is no zephyr but a steady blast, as if a giant fan had been turned on. Your scent goes with it. If that downward thermal drift is of real wind velocity, it fortunately tends to disperse your scent, making it hard for deer to get an accurate fix.

The likeliest time to have a stalk spoiled by thermal drift is when it's so light that you hardly notice it and forget it. That cost me a nice four-pointer in Montana's Gravelly Range late one afternoon. Following a low line of cliffs, I spotted him about three hundred yards ahead and down on the flats, casually feeding. That was stretching the range of my Remington 6 mm, so I wanted to get closer. This required moving away from the too-visible cliff edge. I veered into timber and counted paces to bring me about abreast of the feeding buck below and out from the cliff. Sneaking back to the edge of the cliff, I saw the buck. But he was already turned away to flee, warily watching back over his shoulder as if fearfully expecting to see me. When he did, two fast jumps rocketed him into thick junipers for keeps before I could get the crosshairs on him.

At first I was mystified. My footwork had been too quiet for him to hear me approach that cliff edge. Then I thought of late afternoon downward air drift. The air had felt calm, but when I struck a match, there was a steady warp to the flame right in the buck's direction.

In addition to this upstairs-downstairs thermal drift phenomenon, the hunter also must deal with regular wind. In high country, there's often plenty of it. The frustrating thing is its undependability. High and irregular landforms distort a monodirectional wind into what old sailors called veering and flawing. That is, changing direction erratically. If the wind is blowing around a big land mass like a high peak or even a big butte, it will back-eddy just like flowing water does where a stream bends or rocks distort the water flow.

Fickle winds like this can make life difficult for a hunter trying to approach game. He may start an apparently safe crosswind stalk, only to be horrified one hundred yards farther on that the wind is now on the back of his neck and blowing his scent straight at the quarry. One defense is to glass with binocs and try to detect from grass-top or leaf movements just which way the wind is blowing farther ahead. Again, it always helps to be above the game. Then if your scent is blown ahead of you by a treacherous wind shift, it will likely be above the deer and still rising on a mild day. But conversely, cold winds flowing downward can wipe out your height advantage.

There are other times when with luck you can work downwind on game. One is when the breeze is light and you can see far ahead. If you travel downwind in a straight line, you're "pushing" your scent continuously ahead. But if you zigzag a lot at sharp angles to the wind, you have a chance of not alerting keen-nosed deer well ahead. That is, when you zig into a "clean" sector, it takes a while for your scent to reach a deer well downwind. A 4-mph light breeze takes almost two minutes to broadcast your scent about two hundred yards ahead. If you don't dally, a buck out there can be sized up and picked off in much less time. But a stronger breeze naturally moves your scent ahead faster.

Not always is your scent a tactical embarrassment. Sometimes you can use it to deliberately flush game. I stumbled onto this years ago in Wyoming. Hiking back to camp, I quietly came out on a ridge upwind of and overlooking a minibadlands capable of concealing a hundred deer. I glassed the area awhile, then relaxed and quietly munched a candy bar. Minutes later, I was startled to see sneaking through the gullies a distant buck who turned and stared furtively in my direction.

The only explanation is that my scent alerted him in his peaceful bed in some shady washout in the broken ground. Had I kept going, he might have remained hidden and played the game of letting me pass before sneaking away — or simply stayed put. When well hidden, big muleys can be iron-nerved. But my failure to put in some appearance after several minutes was ominous, and he decided to discreetly ghost out of the area. His ghost may have made it, but he didn't.

Like smoke, scent fans out as it moves. A muley's eyes are very precise. His hearing is fairly accurate — he can tell where a sound came from. But a whiff of scent is relatively vague data. All it tells the deer is that you're upwind there *somewhere,* maybe far, maybe dangerously close. If, lacking sighting or hearing data, he can't pinpoint you any better than that, he is likely to be one ready-to-book-out buck. And a muley on the move is many times easier to spot than one hidden.

Even in the better timbered ranges of the West, there are lots of open lands, often covered with low sagebrush or scatterings of juniper. Usually these are south or west slopes too sun-baked for other trees to grow on. When covering a lot of ground, it's tempting to walk across such open range. But a hunter on foot in the open can be seen a long way by a mule deer and recognized as potential danger. Unless the detour is impractically long, better to cut around such openings by circling just inside the edge of bordering timber.

In hill and mountain country, is it best to stay put or move? That depends on several factors. Given normal weather and early season, spending a lot of time concealed on good vantage points and working your binoculars hard is common sense strategy. If you can get up there very early, you're likely to have other, slower-starting hunters coming up below you. Often they'll flush game uphill your way. This works best where you count on plenty of other hunters being on hand, such as in the heavily hunted national forests of high-hunting-pressure areas like Colorado or eastern Washington's Okanogan country.

A workable plan for a day in the high country is to start in as early and high as possible with hopes that either deer moving on their own or being pushed by other hunters will come your way. In either case, by midmorning the bloom may be off the rose. Deer are likely to be bedded down, and the morning ascents of other hunters have taken place. Now what? This may be the time to start still hunting of the move-little, look-lots variety. In the big, sweeping hills typical of high country mule deer hunting, one is tempted strongly to cover lots of ground in a hurry. Always there's an urge to see as quickly as possible what's over the next ridge. And in good muley range, likely you will move a fair number of deer that way. Many of them will be easily stampeded does or witless forkhorns. But the biggest bucks in their midday concealment are very cagey about letting fast-moving hunters sweep past.

My first (but not last) lesson on this was long ago in Wyoming. Ambitiously, I was covering lots of ground along a ridge bare of cover except sage and a few boulders. Since I was working the heads of all the ravines on the ridge's side slopes, my narrow ridgetop held no interest — wasn't hardly cover enough for a jackrabbit. For some casual reason I looked back over my shoulder and almost had a stroke. Just disappearing over the far side of my ridge was a monstrous muley. Frantically I ran to the same edge and missed him with two hasty shots as he bounded downhill to vanish into a maze of gulleys and high greasewood.

Backtracking, I found fresh droppings and an obvious deer bed alongside an L-shaped rock no bigger than an executive desk. The buck had lain there and gambled on my long-stride passage not thirty yards away. Once I was past, he vamoosed, and a little lead flying slowed him not. An hour's search of the last-seen area showed no blood, hair, or buck.

In those days, that area got little hunting pressure. A mature buck could be careless about bedding. *If* I had moved slowly, it's a strong bet his nerve would have broken. *If* then he'd have attempted a getaway at close range in front of me, he very likely would have ended on the meat pole. And if my aunt was built a lot different, she'd be my uncle.

When spooked, a mule deer's overwhelming inclination is to run uphill. With this in mind, a buck often beds just at the edge of higher timber or rimrock refuge. If he beds up on top where there is no higher ground to flee to, a brushy or rocky knob overlooking a fork, or a Y of canyons is a classic roost for him. He's also very partial to flaking out on a narrow ridgetop with good-cover escape canyons on either side. If trouble comes one way, Mr. Buck barrels out the other route. If his escape route is downhill, you can bet he'll head for the best available cover, be it timber, brush, or deep gulleys. You can also bet that when Condition Red is past, he'll sneak back up to high ground somewhere.

In addition to weather influencing his whereabouts, a mature muley alters his entire lifestyle when season opening brings totally unusual disturbance. Prior to that, the big semisolitary buck in his mountain fastness does not get much human hassle. He may get rousted once in awhile by random stockmen, foresters, or summer hikers. But not often.

In country that gets hunted very much, he's a fast learner. He becomes an excellent tactician if he lives through his first few seasons. Very rarely will he position himself in a sucker situation. He may make that mistake the first day or so of the season. But if he survives an error or two then, he is not likely to make any more the rest of the year. He likely won't come out to feed until well after dark and may go home to bed long before dawn. Only it probably won't be the same pads he was using before the hills suddenly filled up with snarling vehicles and flashy blaze orange. Until real, no-foolin' snows force him lower, he'll bed higher and in better concealment.

Until it's time for the mating game, he'll stay even farther away from herds of does and fawns he normally avoids. He may have stood and gawked at you from fifty yards back when you saw him in August velvet. Now he may not give you five hundred yards of grace and space. He knows the country intimately, which you probably do not. But you have a brain capable of conjecture, which he probably lacks. In sizing up an area to still-hunt, ask yourself where you'd bed down if you were a mature, gun-shy buck. Then, staying out of sight, work yourself above such areas and approach them upwind very slowly, stopping often to burn holes in your binocs with hard looking — at *everything,* including small patches of rock or brush. Look for only bits of a buck — a patch of misplaced black that may be his nose or skullcap trademark. Maybe only his antlers show. (Good tip: In dry weather and decent light, antlers gleam a bit more than similar-looking dead-brush branches.)

Finally, one of the best ways to hunt hill and mountain mule deer is when teamed up with one or more partners. Then you have such options as driving smaller cover areas. One of the best modes is for two hunters to work upwind along high ground with one man low, the other (doing his utmost to use cover) on top. Keep your mouths shut, and use hand signals when necessary. Such signals should be: 1) simple, and 2) agreed upon beforehand.

I still remember a dramatic signal episode. A delightful partner, Jim McFall, and I were working parallel ridges in Wyoming's Powder River breaks with a canyon between us (excellent way to mousetrap any buck who makes the mistake of running away from one ridge to the other). Jim waved both arms to signal "Attention!" Then he began vigorous hand signals that baffled me, including pointing to his backside. I assumed it was something about seeing the rump of a deer running away which was hardly worth all this semaphorical energy on McFall's part. Finally I shrugged and made a long, hot hike down into the canyon and up on his ridge. When I wheezed up to Jim and asked what his urgent signals were, he replied, "All I was signaling was whether you had any toilet paper I could borrow."

10

All-Weather Deer Hunting

Weather's effects on mule deer are described in other chapters, but what about us, the hunters? Can extremes of weather really affect the way we hunt, or is it all in our heads?

Well, try this true nightmare scenario. A big buck is seen. Aim and squeeze trigger. Click. Frantic working of bolt action to chamber fresh round. Click again. Plus two more misfires. Hasty look at ejected live ammo shows primers are indented — somewhat — so it's not a broken firing pin. Finally the fifth round fires and drops the buck who was luckily too far off to hear the rifle action's clatter during the four cardiac-arresting misfires. That happened to me last fall. The cause? A temperature of fifteen below zero congealed WD-40 oil, already gummy with age, on my Springfield's firing pin to where it simply wasn't hitting primers hard enough.

This was pure carelessness. I learned at age nine hunting snowshoe rabbits in subzero that too much oil could put a gun out of action, and ever since had been careful not to apply much to the lock mechanism of any gun used in cold weather. What I didn't realize is that externally applied gun oil can migrate down inside the bolt over the years. Strip down and thoroughly clean the mechanism of any gun to be used in low temperatures (or have a gunsmith do it). If you do use gun oil internally, the modern synthetics like Rem-Oil and Break-Free won't freeze, and their molecular-bonding nature makes them excellent rust protection.

However, use *any* oil sparingly. Sporting rifles don't need lubricant to function, and they are used so little that lack of lube won't cause undue mechanical wear. Any oil will pick up dust in hot, dry weather and become more grinding compound than lubricant. At best, autoloading rifles are never as reliable as manually operated weapons, and a combination of too much lubricant saturated with dirt and crud can be counted on to cause stoppages in autoloaders. They can also jam due to ice sticking to the exposed part of the bolt. That problem cured me of autoloading shotguns years ago.

Far more delicate than a rifle, a scope sight deserves special attention in extreme weather. Nitrogen-filled scopes are advertised as fogproof. Many of them are not. Before mounting a new scope, submerge it in warm water. The warmth will cause the gas inside to expand slightly. Any small bubbles mean the scope's hermetic sealing has been compromised. Take it back to the dealer or mail it to the manufacturer with a complaint, because this baby *will* fog on you in cool, damp weather.

Hot weather itself poses no problem for a scope. But protect lenses from dust with scope covers. In dusty travel, consider zipping the rifle up in a case even if the law doesn't require it. Keep binoculars, cameras, and spotting scopes cased for the same reason. To clean lenses, blow off as much dust as possible. Then remove the rest by very gently wiping with lens tissue or a clean, soft cloth—best kept packaged to avoid dust saturation. Hard wiping will scratch coated glass lenses and murders budget-camera plastic lenses.

Heavy rain or snow menaces scope usage. See-through storm covers aren't the answer. They get covered with snow or rain blurred as much as unprotected lenses. The best bet here are quick-release lens covers. When adjusted properly, the elastic type snap off quickly. But that makes plenty of noise—a disaster when you want to quietly draw a bead on a not-distant animal.

As cited in Chapter 6, quick removal or swing-off of a scope to allow use of iron sights has real merit in bad weather. If it's snowing hard, I remove the scope, stick it in my daypack, and rely on auxiliary iron sights. In a snowstorm, any shooting is likely to be at close range (probably in some cover situation) where iron sights are fine. They're more snowproof than any scope and faster and quieter to get into action than a scope with elastic lens covers. My thirty-year favorite mount here is the rugged, reliable Pachmayr Lo-Swing, which also allows full removal of the scope with return-to-zero on remounting.

More than one gunsmith has told me of customers bringing in rifles with "jugged" or split barrels due to firing when bores were plugged with snow, or more likely, snow that turned to ice. The surefire prevention is simply to put a piece of tape (any kind that sticks) *over* the muzzle. That external obstruction won't hurt anything; it's an obstruction inside the tube that does the damage on firing.

Hunters who wear glasses benefit greatly from going to contact lenses, which are far more weatherproof than regular spectacles. Due to rain smear on his glasses, the most law-abiding hunter I know unintentionally mowed down an illegal doe next to a legal buck.

In hot weather, don't store ammo in a vehicle glove box. Temperature there gets very hot and can bake ammo into higher than usual firing pressures. This may not result in a problem with factory ammo, but I've known handloads that were problem-free in normal weather to start blowing primers and offering sticky extraction under such conditions.

*   *   *

The typical truck camper or trailer is so poorly insulated for cold weather use that even a heating system running full blast may not keep the place very warm. This can be easily remedied with insulation applied to (not within, which would be a real panel-removal problem) out-of-sight interior walls inside sofa-dinette-storage voids and cupboards. In a typical RV, that accounts for a lot of wall area. Just corrugated cardboard helps, and one-inch builders styrofoam is even better. Insulation sheets inside cupboards can be held in place simply by canned goods or other contents. In other areas, use double-sided carpet tape or staples. As a bonus, such insulation helps keep the rig cooler in hot weather, particularly when a shade tarp is rigged over the roof.

Floor warmth is improved by thick carpeting. Leave a couple of windows as is for ventilation purposes, and cover the rest with external storm windows of transparent polyethylene sheeting held on with duct tape. These must be applied beforehand in mild weather, since the tape won't adhere if applied to cold aluminum. Such storm panes cut heat loss through windows and eliminate heavy frost buildup on the inside of glass in cold weather. Finally, add extra weatherstripping to the door. I was amazed at how much difference these simple steps made in my sixteen-foot travel trailer in weather well below zero. Since this winterization tends to seal the unit, be sure to have some window ventilation to prevent any stove monoxide buildup or oxygen depletion.

Also helpful in cold weather is to select a sheltered campsite for either tent or camper placement. Evergreens thick enough to form a

Even a tent this large can be kept comfortably warm if you were to install a modest wood stove. Note snow banked along the bottom of the side panel to shut out cold drafts at floor level. Same trick keeps a trailer warmer.

windbreak and high enough to stop open-sky radiation loss of ground heat can be many degrees warmer than an open area nearby. For a stay of several days, twenty minutes of shoveling to snowbank the bottom of a trailer helps keep the floor warm by sealing off wind flow's convective heat loss underneath.

A cold-weather tent camp needs all the heat-holding help it can get. Snowbanking is useful here, and so is a tarp rigged as an insulative fly. Tent camping in low temperatures need not be life in a deep freeze—a good wood stove can keep you in shirtsleeves. For overnight heat, stoke it with plenty of wood, damped down for slow, long-lasting combustion. Even better is to bring a sack of coal (if logistics permit) for all-night heating. Have some kind of grate in the stove to prevent burning out the stove bottom.

"Cold weather" deserves some definition. A high pressure cell of cold, clear weather is typical in the wake of a snowstorm, and this can occur as early as the first week of October in the West. Often this post-storm cold snap is calm weather, and a well-clad hunter on the move may get too warm rather than suffer from cold. But beware the well-known wind chill factor. That's when exposed tissue such as your face may need protection. Remember that swift travel on a snowmobile generates its own formidable wind chill and resultant danger of frostbite. A facial scarf wrap or ski mask then is vital.

However, even in a dead calm and with all the clothes he can wear, a stationary hunter will get chilly in zero or colder weather. After decades of shivering on deer stands in zero weather, I finally discovered the tin-can charcoal heater. Puncture some side-vent holes near the bottom of a gallon can (for instance a three-pound coffee can) and fill it about one-third full with charcoal. The self-igniting type is hard to get burning in real cold, so I prefer regular charcoal with a generous dash of charcoal lighter fluid. A lot of heat is generated, and hunkering down over that will keep you warm. Wrapping a small tarp around you with the charcoal heater down between your legs will almost cook you even at twenty below.

Glowing charcoal is practically smokeless and noiseless. I doubt if deer consider its woodsy odor as alarming. Who knows—it might help mask your human scent. Heater, charcoal for the morning, and a small amount of starter fluid weigh very little and fit easily in a daypack. This can revolutionize your zero-weather stump sitting.

*   *   *

For cold-hardy hunters, some of the best hunting is in late-season mule deer migrations. In the lower mountains and milder climates of the Southwest, such migrations are hit-or-miss and in places may not even merit the term migration. In their central-northern Rockies heartland, mule deer are highly migratory, moving late in the fall to winter over at lower elevations. Distances traveled may be anywhere from only a few miles to well over one hundred miles in the case of the so-called Interstate Deer Herd that summers in Oregon's mountains and winters in northern California.

Some hunters assume that muley migrations are caused only by heavy snow in high country. Yet other factors include rutting season, decreasing food availability in higher areas, the approach of a major storm, or just the calendar telling them to move. Sometimes these are trickling movements, usually spearheaded by does and fawns. But migrations can be regular processions of deer. Breaking camp once in Wyoming, our hunting party was treated to the spectacle of unusually large herds of up to fifty deer passing within one hundred yards of us in midday, all headed into a wintering valley. Despite our proximity, the deer generally ignored us in their haste to get down-country. Not until twelve hours later did a big storm arrive.

Of course, hunting a migration is a good way to find big bucks flushed out of their high-country hideouts. Although biologists say that mule deer can operate in up to two feet of noncrusted snow, a buildup of sixteen inches is often enough to get them moving. Just a few inches of crusted snow is something deer will move considerable distance to avoid. Unless weather turns really violent, muleys in mountains offering good timber cover may take some days to drop a few thousand feet, feeding and bedding enroute. Bigger bucks may lag a thousand feet or more behind, depending on snow depth and condition, feed availability, and whether the rut is actually underway. Often, big bucks will be hanging around just above the snow line, while lesser deer have moved just below it.

Unless you know in advance of an area that has muley migration routes, it may take a lot of scouting to locate them. Typical migration travel is down sheltered draws, often but not always south-facing ones. Next to knowing where to plant yourself to cover a migration trail, the important thing is to be prepared for hours of staying put in likely cold weather. Bring some extra clothes (for instance, a warm down parka) in your pack.

A big hitch is that some mule deer states don't have seasons running late enough to count on migration hunting unless there has been some unseasonally early snowstorm activity.

*   *   *

For whatever reason, hunters are a conservative lot, never too anxious to experiment. Maybe that's why more western hunters aren't into snowshoeing. The webs can give you snow country mobility you won't have on foot.

A misconception about snowshoes is that they work best in deep, fluffy snow. Actually, they're at their poorest then. Heavier, wet snow supports the webs and your weight far better. Webs can be a godsend when supporting you on snow crust that your feet alone crash through. Breaking trail in snow where you break through crusted surface every step is exhausting. Here, snowshoes can let you shuffle right along atop the crust due to the wider distribution of weight.

Here's an example of where snowshoes would have saved the day. On a late October hunt in a range of the Rockies already hit by a good snowstorm, I left my 4wd pickup and started climbing an open ridge covered with a few inches of uncrusted, no-problem snow. Heading for deer-elk timber cover about a mile distant, I topped over the ridge and had to skirt a big, open basin. Here I ran into trouble. Wind had not blown this basin partially free of snow, and warming-freezing temperatures had crusted the snow. Every step was a crust-breaking struggle. After a few hundred yards, I gave up and returned to my vehicle, cursing my shortsightedness for having left my snowshoes some miles away at base camp.

Next day I returned with my long trail webs and skimmed over most of that crusted-snow basin with no problem. Since there was little snow on the forest floor, I removed the snowshoes on arrival there and left them for retrieval on the way out. A smaller pair of bearpaw webs could have been tied to my pack when I entered the timber, allowing me to hunt a fresh stretch of country back to the truck. However, bearpaws might not have supported me on the crusted snow of the basin route.

Obviously, snowshoe designs are compromises. The smallest are the

A virtue of smaller snowshoes is that you can conveniently backpack them once you're out of deep snow, something that often happens when you're going into timber or dropping to lower elevation.

ovoid bearpaws. Like other designs, they come in different sizes. They offer much less support in soft snow, particularly for an adult male hunter who may gross 230 pounds with his clothes, daypack, and rifle. On the other hand, they're easier to walk with and have a short turning radius—important when switchbacking up steep grades.

Ovoid but with a tapered tail and often a narrower nose section is the Maine/Michigan, Ojibway, or beavertail pattern. In smaller or medium sizes, these allow some overlap walking—that is, the teardrop design lets the wearer keep his legs closer together if his steps are long enough. Also with a tail but more parallel in shape and with turned-up tips is the Yukon or trail design. These can be big shoes, up to fifty-six inches long or more.

Which is best? It's impossible to answer, since it depends so heavily on where and how they'll be used. The turned-up front tip of trail snowshoes is helpful in climbing or descending slopes, and their narrower styling allows better sidehill travel. But they are heavier, more awkward snowshoes. The weight factor is important—the British Mt. Everest expedition of 1953 did some research showing that in terms of energy demand, an extra pound on the foot is equivalent to an extra five pounds carried on your back.

My personal preference is for the classic Ojibway shoe in a medium size. These are a compromise, offering more support than bearpaws with better maneuverability than trail models. Unlike longer versions of trail shoes, they're still small enough to be taken off and carried on a packboard through shallow-snowed timber.

Almost as important as the choice of snowshoe models is picking the right bindings. Your best bet here is to shop for them when you have your boots along to slip on to see how they feel in various bindings.

Recent years have seen snowshoes made of light metal alloys with different types of synthetic webbing in lieu of rawhide. Generally, they're somewhat lighter than traditional wood-rawhide shoes and very expensive so far, although also available in cheaper kit form. They are an improvement over classic snowshoes, but I cannot honestly call them a major breakthrough. The ultimate state-of-the-art snowshoe has yet to be designed and fabricated.

Four important tips on snowshoe use. One, make sure to cover (not plug) your rifle muzzle with tape as described earlier, since you can make book that otherwise when you fall you'll dangerously plus your gun barrel with snow. Two, for hill country use (a certainty for a muley hunter), get snowshoes with gripper devices on the bottom—great or even essential for slopes. Three, a walking staff helps prevent falls—all the more if rigged with a "basket" above the bottom like a ski pole. (In fact, a ski pole is useable.) Four, snowshoes are tiring to the legs until you're trail hardened. To avoid a next-day crippling case of what the early French *courier de bois* eloquently called *mal du raquette* (sickness of the webs), break yourself in with short, easy excursions.

Skiing is another two-legged travel option for the late-season mule deer hunter, offering much better distance-covering and quieter movement than snowshoes. Unlike snowshoes, which I've used since childhood for sport, hunting, and running traplines, I plead *no comprende* so far with today's specialized cross-country skis. Presumably they'd be terrific for making lots of mileage easily. Just the prospect of very quietly moving along miles of snowy back-country forest roads that muleys also use makes me lick my chops. A skier lacks traction to drag game, so quartering or boning out the kill for backpacking would be necessary. However, that's the best system anyway if real distance is involved.

*   *   *

In the quick-change autumnal weather of the high West, keeping track of oncoming weather is important both to your tactical hunting plans and to avoid something disastrous like being snowed in. The surest bet is to get forecasts regularly with a decent AM radio. Performance of both FM and the little radios pretuned for constant-weather-broadcast frequency is nil if you're surrounded by high mountains. In an aluminum camper or trailer, your AM works best with the antenna next to a window.

Always handy is the ability to read weather on your own. Cloud formations are a reliable guide. Remember this useful rhyme:

> *Mares' tails in a mackerel sky*
> *Never leave the ground long dry.*

That's accurate forecasting. "Mares' tails" are the high, wispy clouds that do resemble horse tails extended in the wind. According to *Meteorology for Naval Aviators,* these cirrus clouds "at times serve as the first visible indication of approaching storm." In fact, the naval book quotes a more nautical jingle:

> *Mackerel sky and mares' tails*
> *Make tall ships carry low sails.*

The "mackerel sky" refers to the stippled or fish-scale appearance of high cirrocumulus clouds. If these are followed by the wispy mares' tails, rain or snow is coming, usually in less than twenty-four hours.

Still another one to watch is the cirrostratus formation—a thin, whitish veil covering the sky. Sun and moon will show through these, often with a ring or halo effect. If this changes to a denser, "ground glass sky" obscuring sun or moon even more, only a few hours remain before probably prolonged rain or snow. Everyone should know the towering, anvil-shaped cumulonimbus "thunderheads," which mean lightning, hail, and torrential rain—often plenty of wind, too.

Dark, greasy gray, sun-hiding clouds are nimbostratus bringing significant rain or snow very quickly. By contrast, the pleasant-looking white cumulus clouds like baskets of wool mean good weather. If these start bunching and enlarging upward, rain and/or thunderstorm activity is on the way. At day's end, these may be broken-up or roll-shaped stratocumulus, usually meaning a clear night ahead.

Also accurate is:

> *Red sky at morning, sailors take warning.*
> *Red sky at night, sailors' delight.*

A brilliant red sunrise usually means rain or snow in twelve to fourteen hours. In hot weather, the sun setting as a dull red globe means more hot, fair weather. A colorful lavender and blue sunset promises more good weather but not necessarily hot. Lots of bright golden or amber color in the sunset can be a precursor of high winds next day. What I call a margarine sunset of pale yellow usually means rain or snow coming.

It is useful to remember that fast-changing weather will move on quickly, but a slower change will last longer:

> *Short notice, soon to pass;*
> *Long notice, long will last.*

Campfire smoke is a good barometer. When it climbs readily (perhaps angled by wind), high pressure prevails, which is good weather. If smoke rises sluggishly and then flattens out or settles, low pressure is here, which means wet or stormy weather.

A phenomenon of western mountain country is the chinook wind bringing unbelievably rapid warmup. This is caused by a westerly airmass flow down the east faces of north-south mountain ranges, compressing itself enough to heat up—as any gas does on compression. Tales of temperatures rising a degree a minute over an hour are not farfetched. Once I headed out hunting at daybreak with the camp thermometer reading five degrees. I came back to camp at 11:00 A.M. wearing only my longjohns and boots, carrying what clothes my backpack wouldn't hold, and sweating like a horse in seventy-degree temperatures.

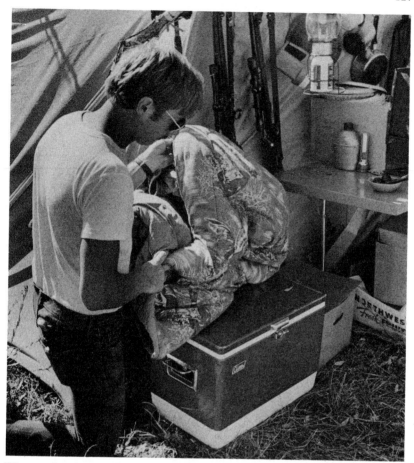

When weather signs say that the air will continue hot, you can take such steps as covering chest coolers with a sleeping bag for daytime insulation. This tactic saves ice and reduces chances of food spoilage.

In remote country, don't take chances on getting trapped by a big storm. Powdery snow is one thing, but on open ridges this can be wind packed hard enough to defy not only 4wd but even heavy equipment. Not long ago some Montana hunters, whose 4wd vehicles were snowbound in the modest-elevation Gravelly Range, at a cost running into four figures hired dozers and finally a backhoe to try to open a wind-drifted exit road. But their vehicles stayed there until late spring.

11

Backpacking and Spike Camping

Even through 7x50 binoculars, my eyes thought my watch was optimistic in announcing legal shooting time. From my high ridge, the benches and flats below were still dim, thanks to heavy cloud cover delaying first light. Fresh out of a warm sleeping bag, I was shivering with the cold as I glassed below. I'd slept okay in this overnight spike camp that amounted to a nylon tarp rigged as an open-faced tent, an Ensolite pad, sleeping bag, a half-empty thermos of now-tepid coffee, and a tiny battery alarm clock.

I was looking for one particular big buck that I'd jumped two days in a row up in the rimrocks and junipers of this ridge. He'd taken off quickly when at several hundred yards he spotted me coming up the too-naked benches below his crow's nest. On the second day, I tried using better cover to work uphill at dawn. But I got very little farther on that attempt.

To get this guy, I'd have to sneak into his bedroom while he was out for dinner—somehow get up on the high ground while he was down in the valley's alfalfa meadows. That's why I was here before daybreak after hiking a long detour up to his bedding ridge in early moonlight nine hours before, gambling that he'd already left to feed. And now the binocs picked up a flicker below. It vanished for agonizing seconds, then reappeared as a five-pointer entering a major draw, as I'd both hoped and expected. As if nervous about not reaching the ridgetop while it was still dark, he walked fast and only took a few minutes to be abreast of and a bit below me. Range—about one hundred yards.

As it often is, the shot was anticlimatic. He never heard it. I put the rifle down and with the dregs of my coffee silently toasted both the dead buck and my overnight bivouac that made this hunt successful. At times I've camped better and at times worse. But scoring on this muley was by far the quickest payoff on big game a spike camp ever provided me.

The great virtue of such bivouacs is to establish the hunter in prime hunting territory without repetitious in-and-out commuting that uses too much time and effort or spooks game en route. Three miles down the valley was my comfortable base camp. But I couldn't operate from there and still intercept my big muley. Certain to see or hear my pickup truck (or me on foot) coming up the valley, he'd either head for the hills well ahead of me or sneak off for the opposite side of the valley where it might take days to find him again. A companion reason for spike camping may be one of sheer logistics. There's a backcountry you want to hunt, but it's hard to get to—impossible to commute there daily from a faraway base camp. So you set up a short-stay camp there on a shoestring basis to keep your gear load light.

Spike camping is ideal for hunting what I call the "no man's land" of mule deer hunting. Most hunters work out on foot from access roads and, frankly, don't get too far. The horse hunters go much farther into backcountry, camping for days. The tactically neglected in-between zone belongs to the backpackers. For simple lack of human disturbance, this zone often holds some nice bucks, and there's lots of it throughout the West's mule deer range.

What's needed for a working spike camp? Not much, if you go back to real fundamentals. Basic camping needs are: 1) shelter from the elements, 2) warmth in sleeping, 3) food and some means of preparing it, 4) water (which can be the biggest problem), 5) a transportation system for this gear plus any game you wind up taking. That system is probably your legs and back, unless you're hunting with horses.

*   *   *

Shelter usually means tent, unless you know of some alternative like a cave (lots of those in hill country, if you include rock overhangs that aren't true caves) or some manmade shelter such as an old miner's cabin or whatever. A problem is that tents today tend to fall into two categories.

One is the big family-sized tent, out of the question for backpacking any real distance. The other is the little "mountain tent," made almost exclusively in low-profile designs to keep them light, cheaper to manufacture, and better able to contend with severe winds at higher elevations. These lack stand-up room to stretch yourself or dress. The majority are two-person models with little storage room for spare gear such as packs and rifles. Space is so limited that you may wind up cooking in your lap, which is a reliable way to burn or scald yourself.

Some years back my oldest son and I bought a mountain tent. As we are both six-footers, our recumbent bodies filled the tent almost completely. Dressing and undressing were highly complex precision drills. We literally slept with our rifles, which with scopes and bolt handles made uncomfortable bed partners. Our packs and food had to be stored outside. To keep that stuff from getting rain or snow drenched required a small plastic tarp along with pious prayer that it wouldn't blow off during the night. Nor did that ease the pain of waking up to a downpour with one's rain gear stashed in a pack outside—meaning getting wet to retrieve it.

Cooking meals with a little one-burner stove is slow at best. Trying to do it inside the glorified pup tent without spilling the pancake mix or syrup in our sleeping bags can only be described as severe colonic trauma. Next time we took along another tarp big enough to rig as a cooking shelter outside. Now we were backpacking not only the tent, frame, and pegs, but also two shelter tarps for gear and cooking, the latter tarp requiring some rope and pegs of its own. Somehow the concept of very lightweight shelter was getting lost. With relief, we sold that undersize nylon coffin to a nonhunting summertime hiker.

Then we belatedly thought hard about what we really needed in a tent. Required was more space for gear storage and to cook a meal inside during bad weather. I wanted some limited standing room, too, because I was tired of doing yoga exercises just to put on my trousers. More space and comfort involved a modest weight penalty, which by now we were willing to pay. That's when we learned how scarce smaller stand-up-room tents really are. Another problem is that most modern tents require some kind of metal pole or fiberglass-rod support system. If you're still hunting on the way in to your spike camp country, you don't want a bunch of aluminum or plastic pole hardware strapped to your backpack to rattle, clank, and catch branches.

I finally came up with an excellent tent. Call it a tall A-style model along the lines of the classic "Explorer" design, which is a very old and good one. It's big enough to dress in while standing erect. It can be entered with only a slight stoop—not crawling on hands and knees. Although designed to use a light T-pole system, it can be easily rigged from a rope between two trees. This little gem weighs less than ten pounds including tent pegs. It is made by Hirsch-Weis under the White Stag label.

In my view, the best factory-made alternative to my tall backpack A-tent would be the Coleman Peak I line's dome-shaped Omega tent. Its forty-eight-inch height lacks stand-up space but offers enough sit-up room for cooking and eating. At seven pounds two ounces including fly and hardware, it's definitely hunter-backpackable. Let's define that term. A backpacking big-game hunter is unlikely to make the mileage of a nonhunting, dedicated hiker. The backpack hunter's range is limited by the highly relevant question of how he's going to get his game out. Even when a sizable buck is boned out, the weight runs a good sixty pounds or more. Much depends on the hunter's age, physical condition, and the kind of terrain to be covered, including whether or not there are trails. There's a big difference between packing eighty pounds on a decent trail in easy country and negotiating very rugged, densely timbered areas with lots of blowdowns or other obstacles. Of course, horse availability is a different ball game, but most pack-in hunters do it on foot.

The tent-product field is a wide one. There are still custom tent and awning shops in many cities that produce a few tents of their own (probably during slack winter season) and also will make a custom job to your specs. Naturally, one of those will be costlier than a mass-production tent. But with today's materials, a good tent should be considered a lifetime investment, or close to it. Nor is it all that difficult to make your own tent.

With that in mind, any hunter seriously interested in lightweight hunting tents suitable for backpacking should consider the old tried-and-true Whelen design. This is simply a lean-to with side panels plus a considerable awning overhang. You can make a small fire under the overhang for sheltered cooking and warmth. That's a convenience not possible with any other tent except the classic tepee with a smokehole. The Whelen in its open mode acts as a reflector oven to a fire directly in front. Bed space is farther inside the Whelen's lean-to portion. In bad weather, the overhang is lowered and secured for fairly weathertight enclosure.

Or you can take a large tarp (nylon for lightness if you plan to pack it far) and rig pretty much the same thing minus the side flaps. I've used a tarp lean-to that way several times. However, add more grommets for better rigging.

With the maximum ventilation of an open-faced tent, use coated nylon for superior rain/snow shedding. Uncoated nylon tenting isn't really waterproof and requires a fly (a de facto auxiliary tent) for genuinely wet weather. Why aren't all tents built completely of coated nylon?

Hunting partner Lee Robinette gets the fire going in a tarp lean-to spike camp that's suitable for mild-weather backpacking.

Because the coated fabric does not "breathe" or exchange air well enough to prevent internal condensation. Just the body heat and exhalation of the occupants will produce enough temperature differential to cause condensation. Additional heat, like a gas lantern, will worsen it.

This can be a real problem. In the haste of World War II, the U.S. Army Quartermaster Corps clean overlooked basic physics when they whipped out a coated-nylon mountain tent design. Despite ineffective tube ventilators fore and aft, these rigs captured moisture inside like you wouldn't believe. These tents were on the military surplus market in the late forties. Not knowing their shortcoming, I blithely bought one and used it — just once, fortunately in summertime. It was like camping with a leaky shower. I went to bed dry and woke up soaked.

A patented textile, Gore-Tex, is both waterproof and air breathing. It's costly stuff, and a tent made of it will run the price of a good, new rifle. But since no fly is needed, a Gore-Tex model is the ultimate in light tenting.

At times I've spike camped with a family-sized aluminum-frame tent.

In one case, two of us had only a mile to go on a flatland trail. Another time we had enough snow to toboggan the tent and other gear on easy terrain. The old-fashioned no-floor wall tent used by many outfitters can make a respectable spike camp when no great backpacking distance is involved and pole material is obtainable on site.

In any tent camping, bring extra ¼-inch nylon cord. It is useful for many jobs, from extra tie-down in stormy weather to pack-lashing game.

* * *

Camping requirement No. 2, decent (warm and dry) sleeping, is simple. For combined lightness plus warmth, a good-quality down sleeping bag is still tops (including price), although some good synthetics have come out in recent years. In mild weather, admittedly you can get by with something less warm. But a lot of backpack hunting for mule deer means going into high country that is usually cold at night in the fall. Then you can't have too warm a sleeping bag.

Various camping books offer tables on bag weight related to temperature. At best, these are crude guidelines. Women or youngsters need warmer sleeping bags, because their smaller size makes them less efficient heat-retaining organisms. (Greater bulk is one of nature's answers to cold-weather survival.) Wearing warm socks and underwear to bed lets you get by with less sleeping bag.

As a very general rule subject to these and other variations, a *high quality,* mummy-style down bag of two- to three-pound content will take care of you down to zero degrees. In my estimation, you can double that bag weight with synthetic-insulation bags. That is, figure on a five- or six-pound bag for the same temperature rating. Some sources add only a fifty percent factor for synthetics, but I think that's optimistic.

A key factor is what you're sleeping on. A decent foam mattress pad provides some limited comfort and vital insulative warmth. Basically, there are two kinds: polyurethane foam, which is open-celled (and thus prone to take up moisture); and closed-cell materials such as Ensolite, which won't absorb water. Choose the latter type, of course.

In either case, a thick bed of evergreen boughs on which to place your mattress pad will give extra comfort and warmth. It also puts your bedding off the ground in case of troublesome rain seepage into a floorless tent. However, to do much good as an auxiliary mattress, a bough bed had better be at least a foot thick (eighteen inches would be even better), because it will mat down greatly with sizable adult weight on it.

A bough bed has some major shortcomings. First, it's a terrible mess inside a floored tent. Second, it takes quite some time and effort to collect the needed amount of small end-boughs. If you try to fudge the job with a lesser number of bigger limbs, it's like sleeping on a woodpile. Third, in some areas the right kind of evergreens aren't to be had. Most firs with stiff, sharp needles are unusable. Junipers and related cedar types are good but require lots of end tips to do the job. Longer-needled pine like ponderosa is okay if trimmed from young trees. This kind of modest pruning will not hurt a tree.

If you want to camp with minimum disturbance in the heart of good game country, skip the bough bed—too much axe noise to collect that many boughs. The alternative is a very slow job of slicing off end boughs with a knife that had better be sharp and kept that way, *or* doing it with a small meat saw. You need one anyway to cut up game for backpacking, and it will work—albeit slowly—to get your requisite number of boughs.

Air mattresses? In quite mild weather, they are fine if you don't mind the packing weight of one thick enough not to spring a leak on you the first night. But if the weather is chilly, an air mattress is just too cold to sleep on.

A final tip. In cold camping, wear a good wool cap when sleeping unless you have a mummy bag with good head warmth. The uncovered head loses too much of your body's sleep-reduced heat. There's an old, physiologically accurate rule among mountaineers: If your feet are cold, first put on a warmer cap.

*   *   *

For backpacking hunting involving both distance and a stay of more than one day, canned food is too heavy. Dried or freeze-dried food must be used. Some general rules apply to freeze-dried camp foods:

1. Serving portions seem to be computed for dieting midgets, not hungry adults. If a package says, "Serves four," figure it really serves two, probably with no second helpings left.

2. Freeze-dried foods require fair amounts of water for preparation—not good provender for a semi-dry camp where water supply is limited.

3. An extra quart-size camp kettle or two will be worth the packing weight when you're preparing a meal of more than one course from freeze-dried foods.

4. Some freeze-dried grub is pretty good eating. Some of it is weird. If you're a finicky eater, you'd better try some spare samples at home to see if it suits your palate.

5. Freeze-dried foods tend to be fat-deficient for anyone hunting

hard in cold weather, when the body needs such extra fuel. In those conditions, an energetic hunter's caloric demand may be almost double what it is normally. I pack along extra margarine or bacon. (Butter spreads too hard when cold and burns too easily in cooking.) Yes, your body can convert some of its own fat reserve for fuel *but* only at a limited rate that may not meet your demands when burning abnormal amounts of energy in cold conditions. Just staying warm in such weather is quite a caloric demand by itself.

6. Be smart and make a day-by-day menu when planning your trip. That should prevent running short of grub or (more likely) packing along too much, which is pointless and tiring. But pay attention to Item 1 above.

7. Don't overlook straight supermarket availability of many dried foods at much cheaper prices than camping-specialty "trail foods." Examples: rice, beans, oatmeal, dried potatoes, noodles, powdered milk, cocoa, and dried fruit. Package such stuff well to prevent waste and messy spills inside a pack.

*   *   *

Water availability is often the biggest single problem in planning a backpack hunt of more than a day's duration. Therefore, plan to hunt only in country that has some water. (If it's totally dry, muleys are not likely to be plentiful there anyway.) Incidentally, *a common mistake in cold weather is not drinking enough water.* That comes from some expert sources including the U.S. Air Force survival school up in the rugged Washington-Idaho border country. Your extra metabolic rate in cold weather requires more fluid intake, or your energy output suffers.

Do not trust *any* backcountry water's purity. (See why in Chapter 15, along with water purification methods.) Aside from spring water of known quality (nonexistent in many areas), the only pure source is fresh snow. This takes time and fuel to convert into water. Compress it into a ball and melt that first. Then add small amounts of snow. If you add too much at once, it can wick up what water is in the bottom of the pan, possibly resulting in burning a hole in a thin-gauge aluminum pan on a hot flame.

Thought must be given to a convenient-sized container to carry water from a nearby source to camp and in which to keep a useful supply there. An open pail of water is a nuisance, since bugs, leaves, and general crud fall into it. Better is a collapsible plastic water jug in a one- or two-gallon size. However, if water freezes in this, it may be impossible to thaw it — obviously you can't heat it on the fire.

With common sense, camp water can be conserved, meaning fewer water-boy chores. Example: save dish-rinsing water for the next meal's dishwashing. In cold weather, cooking utensils need not be washed but can be scraped fairly clean. Any food residue won't spoil and will be absorbed into the next food prepared in the container.

This leads to the burning question (literally) of how you plan to cook. Many small, light stoves suitable for backpacking are on the market. They add extra pack weight, particularly if several days' fuel is needed. Their single burners require more preparation time for a meal of several courses. But when cooking just a simple meal, a stove's quick heat is much faster than laboriously making a camp fire. They also reduce or eliminate the time and noise spent in gathering and possibly splitting firewood. Finally, a small stove is a good heater in even a fair-sized backpacking tent and allows inside cooking in foul weather, with appropriate ventilation, of course.

In an area with a natural wood supply, campfire cookery is feasible, although more work and mess. Commercial fire starters or paraffin are a godsend to make a fast fire in poor weather. As a rule of thumb, evergreen softwoods make quicker fires, while hardwoods make long-lasting fires with better cooking coals.

Collect plenty of dry wood from windfalls or dead branches. Life, liberty, and the pursuit of happiness will be enhanced if you weatherproof this fuel supply with lightweight plastic. I'll spend extra time to gather lots of smaller, dead-dry "squaw wood" rather than make a lot of wood chopping/splitting noise in an area I think holds game. A light folding Swede saw cuts wood faster and quieter than an axe, weighs much less, and is far safer than a hatchet. Even so, a light cruiser axe is usually worth its backpack weight.

On the market are small light-wire grills for campfire cooking, and they're well worth the minor cost and weight compared to precariously trying to balance pots and pans any other way on a fire. Also, a thick cotton glove plus a pot holder or two help avoid burned pinkies in campfire cooking.

Before a camping trip, check on state or federal camping, woodcutting, or fire-building regulations. Except in wet or snowy weather, always use care with fire in the outdoors, whether in timber country or rangeland. Branch-rake or scuff away dry debris around the campfire site. Never leave a fire unattended. A year before this writing, a government agency slapped some campers with a $150,000 bill representing suppression costs in a nasty forest fire allegedly started by their campfire. Try that one on your family budget.

Finally, give thought to lighting at your spike camp. A flashlight of at least two-cell (D size) battery capacity is a minimum requirement. A gas lantern for cooking after dark is great, but with fuel represents several pounds to be packed. Camping suppliers offer small candle-holding lanterns. These are barely okay for finding stuff inside a tent, largely useless outside after dark. The best solution is the old kerosene barn lantern, made in smaller sizes and easy on fuel consumption.

*   *   *

Without some use of a pack animal, a backpack hunter has the job of getting out a deer in one of two ways: drag it whole or pack it out in pieces. Details of dragging and packing are covered in Chapter 16. For real distance and/or rough terrain, a sturdy pack frame is by far the best system.

A pack frame is just what it sounds like—the frame plus a detachable pack—and should not be confused with the smaller rucksacks. If the pack is primarily a single big bag, it probably will hold a deer quarter. If instead it's compartmented into several different sub-bags, it's best to remove it and lash or strap quarters to the frame itself.

The word on pack frames is simple. As with everything else, you get what you pay for. I've seen el cheapos that I wouldn't trust to carry a couple of six packs. My impartial recommendations are the Kelty pack frames in medium sizes, the L. L. Bean Divided Pack and Frame, and Coleman's Peak I pack frame. However, there are many other excellent pack frames among the five dozen makes on the market, some offered in more than one model.

Outlets catering to technical mountain climbers offer superb pack frames for very large loads. Although interesting to elk hunters, these expedition models are more than the backpacking deer hunter needs. No use hauling unnecessary pack-system weight in a size that's also a real impediment in dense timber. Some more expensive pack frames offer optional "shelves" or cargo racks. These simplify load packing and lashing but are not essential.

In selecting a pack frame, look for these features:

1. Sturdy construction, whether aluminum or plastic. (Good frames like Coleman's Peak I embody very tough plastics.)

2. Pay close attention to width, padding, and quality of shoulder straps and belly band. These are skimped in cheap packs, making them much poorer for heavy loads.

3. Study zipper and fastener quality. These, too, are skimped on in cheap pack frames.

4. A desirable feature in any pack-frame system is easy detachability *without* loose locking parts to get lost.

5. Don't choose a pack in a tan or gray color. Elk-rump yellow is unwise, too. If you have a pack in a dubious color, pin on a large swatch of blaze orange, *particularly when packing antlers or deer hide.*

People have different preferences for packing the main weight high or low. On steep descents, I prefer the load carried low on a pack frame for obvious stability reasons. But I'm more comfortable with a high load in climbing or on level going. One thing is universal—loose shoulder straps are tiring to your back and (because they let a heavy load shift fore and aft a bit) a safety hazard as well.

Finally, don't think that it's macho to overload yourself. A fifty-pound load is a lot in rough country except for superbly conditioned hikers. Maybe you can handle more, at least in easier terrain. Just remember that the more the pack weighs, the more vulnerable you are to injury if you take a spill. You don't want your buddies packing out *your* carcass, too.

12

Special Hunting Tips and Tactics

As he slipped upwind out of the thick pines, the young buck was jittery, as his kind often are late in a heavily hunted season. I was pretty jittery myself, thanks to an unfilled tag and only two hunting days left. What drew him was a piece of facial tissue wet with a few drops of urine from a doe in estrus, or heat. Fascinated, he pointed it like a bird dog. Through my scope, I could even see his nose quiver before I started him on his way to the Nelson freezer.

That helped make me a true believer about scents in deer hunting. No, they're not a cure-all. Yes, they can be misused. And there are times and places where some scents' value is low or zero. The main point is that scents work often enough to be worth using.

Checking doe urine is vital for bucks in the fall. That's how a doe's readiness to breed is gauged by her would-be suitor. Apparently it makes little or no difference to mule deer bucks if the doe urine scent is from whitetails. A buck in the rut is no bigot; muley-whitetail crossbreeding occurs where the two coexist. My son shot one such hybrid years ago in Wyoming.

The scent that mesmerized my buck was Tink's #69 Doe-in-Rut Buck

Lure. This is a simple attractant to draw sexually inquisitive bucks. It's not a screening scent to cover human odors. More on those later. It's also not cheap, should not be "cut" with water or other additives, and should be used in fairly copious amounts. Even so, its net cost is a very minor part of a typical deer season's outlay.

Tink Nathan of Safariland Hunting Corp., McLean, Virginia, a veteran bowhunter who sells the stuff, gives explicit advice on how to use it. Get several of the plastic canisters that 35 mm film comes in (try a local film lab). Be sure to wash these inside *thoroughly* to kill the pungent film smell. Then stuff with tissue or cotton balls. Pour doe urine atop this, then cap the canister. Where you plan to take a stand, uncap six to eight of these "scent bomb" canisters in strategic spots for broad-spectrum coverage. The idea is to broadcast that doe-urine odor downwind into areas you suspect or at least hope contain a buck. But do not place it directly downwind from where you are. When a buck is homing in on the scent, you don't want him to see or smell you just beyond it.

Do *not* leave the scent system behind when you depart the area. The only time you want a buck investigating Ah, Sweet Mystery of Life here is when you're on hand to emcee the surprise party. This rules out pouring the stuff on the ground or foliage from which a buck may learn in your absence that it's not worth checking out again.

Effective range downwind varies greatly. Without wind to carry it, scent's effectiveness is zilch. Hot, dry weather limits animals' scenting ability. How much? I don't know, but if deer scenting ability is somewhat comparable to bird dogs, my guess is fifty to eighty percent reduction. Strong, erratic winds probably diffuse scent so much that it can't be smelled very far away—maybe fifty to one hundred yards. Best use plenty of it then. Heavy rain or thickly falling snow prevents scent spread. Cold or frozen urine produces almost no odor.

But under *good* scenting conditions, the range of doe urine may be several hundred yards. Jeff Nathan of Safariland has used their #69 doe urine in mule deer hunting and got one buck that clearly responded from a three-hundred-yard distance. My guess is that could be exceeded. An assumption by some wildlife biologists is that evolutionary selection of mule deer in open country makes them more dependent on their eyes, less dependent on scenting than forest whitetails and blacktails. Even so, mule deer have demonstrably excellent noses. When it was impossible for them to have seen me, my human odor once alarmed a herd of muleys at 400 to 450 yards in warm, dry weather not ideal for scenting.

In open country, scent carries farther than in forest where brush and trees break up wind flow and dissipate scent. In warm, dry periods, use sex scent early in the day. Scent transmits best in moderately cool, high-humidity weather. Fortunately, such conditions often prevail in the autumnal West after hot weather is done.

The best doe-urine results might be when muley bucks roam a lot *before* the rut peak. Although bucks tend to stay apart from does earlier, by fall they are wandering to search out does' home range. They should be inquisitive then. Later, when a buck has several does to tend while trying to keep rival bucks away, he is less likely to wander off investigating just an odor.

The alternative attractants are food-based ones. Of these, I'm skeptical. Mule deer in their home range know very well where the best foods are and may lack interest in substitute scents. Go ahead and experiment, but skip totally "foreign" attractant scents. Don't expect mountain, rangeland, and desert mule deer who've never seen or smelled an apple in their lives to respond to apple odor.

*   *   *

Masking scent is the chemical equivalent of radar jamming. For example, the buck I described that was drawn to the doe urine normally might have been kept away by human scent lingering in the area. The afternoon before, my son and I built a crude tree stand because the forest was too open for ground-level trail-watching. For three hours, our sweaty presence contaminated the area.

When we left, I put out skunk scent to overwhelm our residual smell. When I hiked in next morning, then walked over to the bush where I deposited the urine-scented tissue, I wore skunk-scented pads on my boot soles. As described, the buck homing to that doe scent had no exposure to human odor, or I'd never have seen him. Also, tracks showed nighttime deer not only passed through but stopped and milled about. I'm convinced all that deer activity took place only because the skunk scent suppressed any human odor. Why didn't it mask the doe-urine scent? Probably because I placed the doe scent off beyond the previously skunk-scented zone—which by then had weakened for twelve hours.

Fox urine is another coverup for human odor, although it is not as potent as skunk scent. Both are commercial items—you don't have to dissect a skunk on your own. The latter stuff is frightfully potent. Spillage on clothes, camp gear, or in a motor vehicle would be true disaster. A synthetic called Skunk-Skreen is a binary compound in two containers, individually not offensive and safer to pack around. (In separate pockets, right? Right!) Blended together on a twig or rock, it's an eye-watering replica of genuine eau de polecat.

Like other animals, humans spread scent three ways. One way is through our body (plus our food-tobacco-shaving lotion) odor, broadcast as an indescribably fine aerosol. Another is scent from our bodily functions — a smart hunter never urinates or defecates in a good hunting area without thoroughly covering it with earth or snow. (The easiest way is to kick out your deposit-hole first.) A third way is through scent deposited where we walk. This is partly human odor fallout combined with the smell of our footgear and lower apparel such as trouser legs. How long it lasts depends on atmospheric and other conditions. A chap in my area who uses Bloodhounds to find lost people says human scent often can be followed by the dogs twenty-four hours later. I suspect a deer's scenting ability matches or even surpasses the legendary Bloodhound nose — deer seem to be able to smell stuff from farther off than the hounds can.

Is game spooked by a human-scent-contaminated trail where a hunter has walked? My answer is firmly yes, *if* we're talking about cautious-to-paranoid game like mature bucks. I can't prove that by scientific method, but I am convinced from long experience hunting mule deer, whitetails, blacktails, and elk. Only by being habitual pessimists do those elusive male cervids reach maturity. My conviction is that a grown buck finding human scent trails is likely to avoid that area for a while if he's been spooked by hunting in the past.

So it may well pay a hunter working the same area day after day to chemically "cover his tracks" by using a powerful masking scent. For walking short distances, the use of slip-on foot pads such as Safariland sells is recommended, adding your choice of scent. Since no sane person wants to dribble skunk scent on his trouser cuffs, the alternative to slip-on foot pads is to tie a short length of spare boot lace to your lower leg. At the loose end, firmly tie a piece of rag. Anoint this with skunk scent and mask your own scent as you move. When you leave the hunting area, simply slice off the end of the drag cord rather than mess with it manually.

One excellent deer-elk hunter I know carefully rolls his hunting jacket in a horse saddle pad every night. He reeks horse, and since deer don't fear hayburners, he can stalk game downwind. But for nonhorsemen, the Nathans and other scent experts warn that even good scent technique may not cover certain stenches. Smoking has more potent odor than straight human scent. Also avoid garlic, onions, alcohol, after shave, hair dressing, and so on. Change underwear often, since that's where much of our body smell accumulates. Some killjoy even recommends no meat eating before and during hunting season to avoid smelling like a carnivore. Wouldn't it be tragic for us steak-chompers if he's right?

Personal cleanliness is less scent-productive. An unbathed hunter ripened by days in a camp reeking of fried onions or bacon must be an olfactory cinch for even a deer with acute sinusitis. Masking scent may be at its highest value then. My own rule is that when I start smelling better *with* masking scent than without it, it's time to head for civilization and a shower.

*   *   *

A critical time for caution about your scent is in stalking — not to be confused with still hunting (see Chapter 8). The stalk involves making an approach to game, close or far, already located — more or less. Due to many variables, every stalk is a law unto itself. But here are some general rules.

The most reliable stalk is on game unaware of you. Try to keep it that way! Always best is an upwind stalk. Next best is stalking with the wind at a right angle. Since an abrupt wind switch is possible, it's smart here to be protected by a good masking scent explained earlier. The reaction of a big buck to human scent depends on several factors. A deer living on an active ranch smells people too often to freak out every time. Sometimes a scent-alerted muley takes cover to watch for visual sign of a suspected intruder. When a buck you're stalking suddenly vanishes, that may be what he's doing. If both cover and your stalking technique are good, you may yet be able to pull it off.

By contrast, a hunter-wise buck in remote country is more likely to immediately flee human odor. Unlike ranch deer used to people mending fence and moving cows, the back-of-beyond buck may have known only hunters and the whiplash crack of bullets. The bottom line is to somehow keep the quarry from picking up your scent.

Where blaze orange is required, keeping out of sight of sharp-eyed muleys not yet aware of you requires real finesse. Don't keep popping up for another look at the quarry. Instead, memorize its location, stalk *that,* and avoid the risk of playing too much peekaboo until you think you may be close enough for shooting.

An otherwise perfect stalk can be ruined by unexpectedly jumping other deer. Typical of herd animals, mule deer react instantly to alarm by other game, including panicky rabbits. Before starting your sneak, look carefully for potential tattletales. I once had a promising stalk of a peacefully grazing big muley blown by an unforeseen antelope. When the scared pronghorn raced past with its rump flared in the classic alarm signal, the deer asked no questions but took off at high knots too.

If starting to stalk a deer on the move, try to anticipate where it's headed. If the animal is distant and moving, be realistic about whether you can catch up — mule deer are fast walkers unless slowing down to feed en route. If your buck is with other deer, beware that muleys on the move sometimes double back to eyeball their back trail.

When game is aware of you, stalking is still possible if you're devious enough. First, be prepared for a longer stalk, often a big semicircle to close in from an unexpected direction. *Always remember that it's best to approach mule deer from above, not below.* A frequent opportunity in range country is when a distant deer is seen from a motor vehicle. The temptation is to halt immediately to begin a stalk. But seeing the vehicle coming to a stop usually convinces a mature buck to go elsewhere. Better that you keep driving. Then, beyond sight of the animal, stop and make a stalk back. At the time the deer is first sighted, pay close attention to where he is *and* his likely escape area—timber or nearby canyon cover. Work those out if the animal has vanished by the time you get back to his last known site.

Although game often has trouble recognizing a horseback rider, a deer sometimes wises up instantly on seeing the rider get off, particularly at closer ranges. Either ride to some cover to dismount or lean forward and slowly slide off on the side of the horse *away* from the suspicious game.

Ever hear the term "stalking horse"? It can work. A hunting partner of mine noted that a big ranch muley had learned (as they sometimes do) that a horse with rider was bad news. Smiling archly, Crafty Hunter walked on the far side of a halter-led horse in a long, diagonal approach to the trophy's favorite rimrock aerie. Alas, with four shots he missed the deer. Whether or not the buck thought the horse did the shooting, it henceforth stayed at least half a mile away from *all* horses, even those without riders.

*   *   *

Next to his boots and rifle/scope combo, a mule deer hunter's best friend is his binoculars. Yet these are probably the least understood hunting gadget in common use.

The dual number of binoculars, such as 7x35, refers first to the magnification (seven times that of the naked eye in this case), and the diameter in millimeters of the objective lens (the big ones at the far end). The latter is a rough guide to light-gathering power. Example: 7x50 binocs give a brighter image in poor light than equal-magnification 7x35's.

Neither number reveals the field of view—how much area the binoculars are covering at a given range. For this, read manufacturer specs listing field of view in feet at one thousand yards. Typical 7x35s have a field of about 350 to 380 feet, okay for hunting open country, although a

Long a favorite of western big game hunters are 7x35 binoculars, a good compromise of magnification, light-gathering power, bulk, and weight.

wider field is slightly more convenient. Similar binoculars rated as "wide angle" have about a 450-foot field at that range. In the visual confusion of close-range timber, you need as wide a field as possible, and the twenty-five percent broader view of wide-angle binocs may save the day.

Traditional for hunting are 7x35s and 8x40s. But their bulk often is unhandy hanging around your neck to clink against your rifle when you're trying to be quiet, or worse, flop up to knock your teeth loose when your horse suddenly decides to leap a log or small stream. The alternative of continually taking them out of a side-slung binocular case, then wrapping up their neck strap to replace them again gets tiresome. Guess what happens then! You gradually quit using them and thus may miss important game sightings.

That makes a strong argument for the so-called compact binoculars, typically 7 to 8X with 24- to 28-mm objectives. These little gems can be left around your neck but tucked into a breast pocket or slipped inside your shirt or jacket. In the dim light of the first or last few minutes of the day, they're not quite as good as brighter-image 35- or 40-mm binocs. But they're far more useful all the intervening hours and are lighter weight in the bargain. Even handier are quality monoculars — singleton optics used with only one eye.

Bigger binoculars starting with 7x50s are on the heavy side for the foot hunter and bulky enough to be a nuisance on horseback. They're fine for vehicle use. Yet here the vote goes to the almost fifty percent extra magnification of 10x50s. The smaller field of 10X is not critical for long-range purposes, which is how binoculars typically are used from a vehicle. A 10X glass naturally is more useful than lower powers for sizing up trophy heads and can be effectively hand held with care. The really far-out head hunter, convinced his manhood is lost if he doesn't make the record book, still needs a 20X spotting scope and a small tripod.

Budget-priced binoculars never last long before mechanically going out of whack with loss of collimation or optical alignment. When that happens, the double-imaging effect is a terrific eyestrain for most users. If your budget won't take much strain of its own, consider buying a good monocular — its single optical system can't get out of collimation.

On the other extreme, the practical value of very expensive binoculars is dubious. The extra cost of producing flat-field, sharp-to-edges fields of view is a bit silly when our own eyes are sharp only in a tiny one-degree field. Fix your eye on one word of this sentence — now notice that all the adjoining words are *not* in focus! It's the same thing looking through magnifying optics — your own vision is sharp only in one small, centered zone. On the subject of reasonable sharpness. I have yet to see any variable-power binocs that cut the mustard here, although "zoom" rifle scopes have much merit.

Rubber-armored binoculars are theoretically sturdier, but all optics deserve careful handling. You can "armor" regular binocs with some judicious wrapping of foam rubber weatherstripping around the rims of the objective lenses and the thickest part of the body if utility is more important to you than appearance. The most convenient binocs are those combining center focusing with individual focusing on just one eyepiece. If that's the left one, first focus with the center post control for your right eye. Then close the right eye and adjust the left-eyepiece focusing. A good trick now is to wrap the latter with a couple turns of black vinyl tape to keep it at that setting. Henceforth, you need only focus with the center post control or lever for fast use in the game field.

If you wear glasses, carefully shop for binoculars that work best in conjunction with your spectacles. Better binocs have fold-down rubber collars on the eyepieces for bringing them closer to your glasses, but

Hearing is highly important in timber hunting, but many males have lost much of theirs by middle age. Today's small hearing aids, such as this one, help to compensate.

there's still a reduction in field of view. Binocs are best held with both hands, although with compacts you can pinch hit with one hand. Holding the glass, brace index fingers and thumbs against forehead and cheek-bones for added steadiness. Now hold upper arms and elbows against your body. If glassing a wide area, do it by individual segments; it's too easy to miss detail if you do a continual sweep, and it's harder on the eyes, too.

$$*\qquad*\qquad*$$

High technology's latest gift to hunters are "big ear" hearing devices. Not to be confused with ordinary hearing aids, these are battery-powered systems that electronically enhance sound thirty to forty times. That can be helpful to the hunter of any forest game, including timber muleys. Like many gadgets, these are aids, not wondrous breakthroughs. While it can be tactically useful to eavesdrop a deer scuffing through the woods one hundred yards away, hearing the critter doesn't automatically mean you're going to see him, let alone get a bead on him. Also, the drawback of any hearing enhancement is that *all* sounds, including jets overhead or noisy logging trucks half a mile away, are amplified. These "electronic ears" are hand held, meaning that holding the sensor ties up one hand to the detriment of possible fast shooting in timber.

Many adult male humans have hearing problems. You may be surprised how much if you have yours tested by a hearing specialist. As years passed, I congratulated myself on how much quieter I'd learned to move in timber. Truth was, a lifetime of serious hobby shooting had cost me about half my hearing. A good hearing aid told me how much noise I was *really* making on the prowl, and I had to take greater pains to be truly quiet. For this reason alone, a hearing aid is highly useful for many timber-brush hunters. As a bonus, it can pick up the sound of game movement you might not otherwise hear. And yes, it's easy to turn off when friend wife says this is the weekend to put up storm windows rather than go hunting again.

13

Friends on All Fours

The first thing to understand about horses is that most of them are stupid, and *all* of them are powerful. That imbalance of no brains and all brawn is an uneasy one. But they're still the big-game hunter's best friend.

Horses are used three ways in mule deer hunting: first is to use the horse as a taxi to go to where you dismount and hunt on foot; second is to use the horse to hunt from; and third is to use the horse for packing gear or game. Most hunters are concerned only with the first two, since the guide-outfitter normally handles horse packing. A horse can cover twice the miles per day of a walker—or much more than that in steep country. You need not be an experienced rider. One Montana outfitter tells of a client so petrified of his docile nag that they had to be halter-led by the guide. Even so, the dude had a good hunt in mountain country, bagging both a nice muley and an elk.

Unless you own horses, your mount will be furnished by an outfitter. Be honest with him about your experience or lack thereof. That's his guideline about what kind of horse to give you. The right footgear (see Chapter 3) has much to do with whether you come back sitting *in* the saddle, or belly-down over it. Never put your foot into stirrups all the way to the arch; if you fall or get thrown, you want your feet to instantly leave the stirrups to avoid being fatally dragged.

Wear the right clothes. Weather dictates this in part. So does the horse. A wind-flapping poncho, as I cited in Chapter 3, can spook a horse. Vinyl rain garments get torn instantly when Noble Steed drags you through snagging tree branches. Riding can be chilling in cold weather, so dress warmly. You probably don't own chaps, but a pair of canvas duck-hunting trousers are next best for brush protection or keeping your legs dry in rain and snow. Small binocs are okay around the neck *if* slipped inside your jacket to keep from flopping. Larger binoculars must be put in a saddlebag along with other gear such as a camera. Don't hang such stuff from the saddle horn. In open country, a wide-brimmed hat is good sun or rain protection but is a nuisance riding through timber. A billed cap is hard to beat. A pair of the small zip-shut nylon backpacks students use for carrying books can be rigged as economical but excellent saddle-bags.

Pay attention when your outfitter saddles your horse. It's wise to at least know how to tighten a saddle cinch by yourself if it loosens during the hunt. Find out if this horse can be mounted from either side. Western horses normally are mounted from the left, but it's better if you can use

In steep country, riding a horse multiplies the mobility and mileage of the mule-deer hunter.

either side as terrain demands. On steep ground, never mount from the downhill side.

The length of stirrup straps greatly affects your comfort. Stirrups too short will produce crippling knee cramps in an unhardened rider. The rule of thumb is: standing in the stirrups, you should be able to pass a clenched fist between your buttocks and the saddle.

On level ground, a horse's center of gravity is about four inches behind his withers (shoulder tops). Try to carry your weight over that area. Most beginners sit too far back. Another mistake is to slouch in the saddle. That's hard on both you and the horse. For the animal, the least-tiring rider is one with enough natural balance and sense of rhythm to ride *with* the horse rather than be dead weight. (When it comes to endurance, a pack horse can't carry inert cargo as far as it can a heavier but more resilient rider. When the Army still used horses, regulations set 175 pounds as a maximum load for pack horses. And that brings up the baffling question of why more outfitters don't use donkeys as pack animals, or even for riding. A 500-pound jackass can carry 250 pounds all day without pain or strain—I've seen it done—in rough country, is far more surefooted than any horse, costs less to buy and feed, and is more disease- and injury-resistant. They *are* slower-paced. But outside of Canada and Alaska, most pack-string trips are relatively short ones.)

However, shift your weight back when your horse is going down a grade. With the reins, hold his head high then. If he stumbles, you can help check him from a real fall or forward somersault. Conversely, shift your weight far forward when the animal is going steeply uphill. A trick an outfitter taught me is to keep reins slack then, lean forward, and grab a handful of mane with the spare hand. That, he said, helps the horse climbing a steep grade, and so it seems to.

Stay laterally centered at all times. If you slouch to one side or the other to ease your aching butt, you give the horse an aching back. Don't ride with your feet stuck out awkwardly. They're more vulnerable to getting caught in brush when that way. Also, you'll stay in the saddle better if more of your legs are in contact with the horse. Keep the reins lightly but securely held. Decent saddle horses don't need much reining to turn them—there is no need to jerk the horse's head off. In fact, ask your outfitter if the horse neck-reins, and have him show you how.

Evolving as plains animals, horses are not as surefooted in broken country as donkeys or half-donkey mules whose wild ass ancestors were mountain critters. When the going gets bad, dismount and lead the horse. Don't leave the rifle in the scabbard for him to fall on. When leading him downhill, stay off to one side so that if he falls forward, you're clear.

Horses are usually good at sizing up riders. Early in the game, make it clear to the horse that *you* are the head field hand. After a summer of ferrying timid dudes on trail rides, outfitters' horses are often used to having things their way. On one hunt, I was assigned a little pinto mare who wasn't at all sure this trip was necessary. I snapped off a pine bough as a quirt and gave her some vocational counseling. From then on, we had a cordial understanding — we did things my way. A couple times when I reached up only to push pine boughs away from my head, she thought I was getting another quirt and quickened pace to show me that *wasn't* needed with a wonderfully attentive horse like her.

By our phlegmatic standards, horses are real spooks. They can't take even harmless surprises. My hunting chum Bob Nelson once was leading a string of riders and pack horses in the Cascades when a herd of elk stampeded past the procession. Although these mountain nags had seen elk all their lives, they exploded. Airborne riders soared in all directions along with pack cargo. Jim McFall for years had a horse obsessively fearful of anything white. Just the sighting of white road signs or a flock of sheep touched off riot and civil disorder, starting with Big Red invariably launching Jim into high, graceful orbit.

Ask your outfitter about any peculiarities of the horse you're using. Find out if your mount has an ongoing feud with another horse of the string, so that you can keep them apart. They're highly individualistic animals. Some are leery of things that other horses ignore. All of them are afraid of bears and snakes. It's wise to stay away from the rear of a horse. That's where the main battery cuts loose if the horse is startled or irritated. Up front, they can bite well.

After dismounting in the field, tie your horse to a tree with a neck halter rope both short and tied high enough that the horse can't trip and tangle a leg in it. If caught that way, a horse panics and can practically saw its leg off. Don't rein-tie it; reins often can't anchor a horse determined to bust loose.

Unless you've done a lot of prehunt riding, hours in the saddle will make you very sore. Dismount and lead the horse about ten minutes in every hour, getting your muscles and cartilage back to normal working modes. This rests the horse, too. Prehunt exercising involving lots of knee bends will save you a lot of discomfort that otherwise can mar a great hunt. Use of sore-muscle liniment like Ben-Gay can help when day is done. A hot, muscle-relaxing bath is wonderful if it can be arranged. On a week-long hunt, Day 2 will be the worst. Day 3 won't be bad at all, and by Day 4 you'll feel fit enough to keep up with Genghis Khan.

God designed horses, men designed rifles, and there wasn't any interdesign consultation. Any mode of carrying a rifle on a horse leaves much to be desired. First, never ride with a round in the chamber. Don't even dream of carrying the rifle slung across your back. It's hazardous to both you and rifle if you fall, and going through timber, that upthrust barrel catching a branch will snatch you clean off the horse. Best is a moderately light rifle with no more than a twenty-two-inch barrel. A long-barreled rifle is too slow to get out of a scabbard fast. With a heavy rifle on a round-backed horse, you wind up exerting tiresome stirrup pressure to offset the rifle weight's pull-down of the saddle. Your horse artillery had better include a top-quality, most ruggedly mounted scope, because nothing is harder on scope zero than days of riding. Keep your rifle scope-up in the scabbard.

When using the horse just to get to where you start foot hunting, the so-called trail or bucket position is best for rifle and scabbard. This is up

Author and his guide during a combo hunt for mule deer and elk in the northern Rockies, take a lunch break and rest their indispensable horses.

Smaller, slender rifles are best for horseback hunting. Author considers this Savage 99 in 284 Win. the best saddle rifle ever made. It has plenty of cartridge power combined with the slender handiness of the lever action. This rifle fits into a much shorter scabbard than this outfitter-supplied version.

ahead of the rider's right leg, scabbard at an angle, and, I hope, not banging into the horse's right front leg, which is not good for rifle or horse. Expert riders with short rifles can swing out of the saddle with one hand while retrieving the rifle right over the horse's back with the other. We inexpert riders are all too likely to tumble doing this, either dropping the rifle in the process or leaving it in the scabbard while a fall-startled horse probably takes off with it. Slung in this upright position, scabbard and rifle are wide open to rain and snow unless you use a scabbard hood — another barrier to fast rifle handling.

Therefore, if riding to find game to shoot quickly, have that scabbard on the same side you're likely to dismount from *and* down where you can grab the rifle fast. Hang the scabbard on the left side, butt up to rear, at about a forty-five-degree angle to keep it from falling out when going uphill. If the horse suddenly moves forward as you dismount, all you have to do is grab the rifle for the quickest one-horsepower scabbard draw of your life. This "hunting scabbard" mode has your left leg over the scabbard and rifle, so the thinner the rifle, the better.

Don't leave the slightest bit of sling loop sticking out to snag on a tree from whence your rifle will be left hanging as you and Ol' Paint ride on. After wending through thick lodgepoles, I dismounted to find my scabbard empty. Riding back, I was very lucky to find my beloved 284 Savage 99 (best saddle gun ever made) nicely hanging from a lodgepole snag. Remove the sling and stick it in your saddlebags.

If planning a horse hunt, get your own scabbard to fit your rifle in case your outfitter can't supply a decent one. The bad news is that quality leather scabbards cost a few hundred dollars and beat the tar out of your rifle. The rough-surfaced leather interior, in a week's hunt, will do things to rifle bluing and stock finish that will make a gun lover moan piteously. Apply several layers of paste auto wax on the weapon beforehand for some limited protection.

Or better yet, buy an intelligently designed modern scabbard. The good news is that Michael's of Oregon has come out with a line of nylon scabbards padded with moistureproof foam that won't chemically react with the gun's bluing — another drawback of leather scabbards. This is the best news since stirrups were invented, and the price is a fraction of a leather scabbard. They're also softer than leather scabbards, which both your leg and the horse's rib cage should appreciate.

When dismounting to walk awhile, have lunch, or whatever, slip your rifle out of the scabbard and keep it with you. First, you never know when you'll see game. Second, horses often get excited when the hunters do, and when you're trying to grab a scabbarded rifle, your horse may be dancing a polka just out of reach or taking off fast for the ranch. If a horse decides to celebrate your absence from the saddle by having a good festive roll on the ground, a scabbarded rifle is a goner.

Never try to shoot from a horse. Even those used in hunting will rarely stand for that. Some use even dismounted gunfire as an excuse to vanish. Ask your outfitter in advance what to do if a game shot presents itself without time to halter-tie the horse. One told me, "Well, I flatly promise that a runaway horse is a lot easier to find again than a scared-off trophy buck or bull elk."

In country with scattered stands of timber, one excellent horse-hunt tactic is for a couple of riders to approach the timber. One dismounts, the other discreetly takes both horses around to the upwind side where he ties them, dismounts, and stays close to them so that their powerful odor, he hopes, cancels out his scent. Allowing time for that posting, Hunter No. 1 makes a foot drive, or still hunt, through the timber. A muley buck typically deciding on distance as his shield will barrel out the far side right into the crosshairs of Hunter No. 2.

With fantastic vision, hearing, and sense of smell, horses are better game spotters than any pointer. When your horse suddenly perks its ears and stares fixedly, look sharp—it's spotted something, often at incredible distance. Could be other horses, or game. On a bitter day in the Bitter-roots, I was riding with my face hunkered into my collar to fend off frostbite. Suddenly the horse stopped and stared ahead. Looking hard, I could barely make out a distant gray form in intermingled evergreens and serviceberry clumps. I glassed it as a decent muley buck. The buck was watching us narrowly, too. But another advantage of the horse in hunting is that game usually (not always) regard horses as harmless and simply don't recognize a rider. After the buck relaxed and went back to browsing on serviceberry, I slid myself and the 284 loose, sat down, and filled my deer tag. It was almost too easy, thanks to the horse not only getting me there but spotting the game for me and hauling it out in the bargain. That kind of full-service deal makes up for a lot of sore rump and stiff knees.

14

Making Hunters in Your Family

All hunters know that luck is important. By far, my best luck in the hunting field is to have had offspring and a wife who enjoy hunting and make great companions. In an age when traditional family structure is taking a beating, those with such common ties as mutually enjoying outdoor sports have strong bonds.

But there's such a thing as helping make one's luck. Over the years, I worked at teaching my family members to enjoy the outdoors, including deer hunting. And I'm very happy to relate what I did and learned along the way—hits, runs, and errors.

First, ask yourself if you really want a spouse as a hunting companion. For some, the honest inner answer is no. I've known a couple of good men and true who took their wives hunting while regarding the little woman as mildly annoying excess baggage. That is, they'd have been secretly relieved to leave the wife at home. The wives sensed this and under those awkward circumstances could hardly enjoy the hunts. Since it is rarely part of human nature to suffer in silence, the result was a self-fulfilling prophecy. It *did* prove to be a poor idea to take the wife along: "She did nothing but complain the whole time." Can you blame her?

Best hunting luck of all is to discover early a possible great partner for life. This father-son team, Ed and Eddie McLarney, were out for deer in Washington state.

Nor is it always a matter of a hunting husband and (to begin) a nonhunting wife. In one case I know of, a single woman was a hunter, thanks to membership in a family of hunters. She then married a non-hunter. They handled this very well. She asked him if he'd like to take up hunting. If so, she would be delighted. If he didn't, that was fine, too, but she still would continue to go hunting at times with her parents and siblings. This was honest communication, not feminist defiance on her part. New husband opted to give hunting a try and liked it. Since he's a fine guy, all the clan's hunters were pleased to have him in the ranks, starting with me—he's my son-in-law.

Second question: Does the spouse really *want* to be involved in hunting? If she (or he) does not, it's a mistake to shanghai him or her into it. Sometimes the reaction is honestly "I don't know. Maybe I should try one hunting trip first to find out." Fair enough.

A spouse with no outdoors background can become an excellent outdoor type even starting later in life. For various reasons, my wife didn't have a clear track to spend time with me outdoors until she was well into her forties. But this proved to be no barrier in her learning and enjoyment, even though her original background was as an eastern city girl.

First, I checked her out to see if she really wanted to take up hunting. This was more than just a do-you-or-don't-you question. We discussed it. I told her very frankly that while hunting could be and should be enjoyable, it could also be hard work, sometimes under trying conditions, such as bad weather. This she knew from my firsthand reports all along, but I wanted to remind her that it was not all sunny days and tires that never went flat in the middle of a snowstorm on a mountain pass. If she didn't feel up to it, fine. If she wanted to join in, even better. That didn't mean she was obligated to go every time. And there would be times when I wouldn't invite her due to expected unusually tough hunting—like lots of horseback riding, which she doesn't dig. Jackie replied, "I want to do more camping, and will you really teach me to shoot?"

This brings up the question about whether the person wants to join the hunt as a nonshooting member *or* fully participate—which means psychologically prepared to kill game. Some people never are, which is no black mark against them. (Don't lump nonhunters with antihunters.) If your spouse genuinely wants to hunt, provide her/him with a personal weapon after initial training. Psychologically this seems to somehow seal the deal. It's important. But from the outset, you have the responsibility of safe training.

We began her rifle schooling, oddly enough, with a 22 handgun. I had reasons for this choice—it is light for a beginner to handle, has almost no recoil and a mild report. First came some explanation, using

Juanita and Sonny Mower, wife and husband from Wyoming, have been a hunting team for many years.

pencil sketches, of the sight picture and target. Next, some dry firing (no ammo) practice. This familiarized her with trigger pull and sight-picture alignment. From the outset, safe gun handling was explained and repeatedly stressed. No deviations from safe procedures were permitted to pass without instant correction.

Then came live ammo. She wore ear protectors for this despite the relatively weak bark of a 22 handgun. Again, scrupulous muzzle control was observed at all times. After the first few shots, the target was scored. We discussed the need for trigger squeeze versus pull. Fundamentals of body and feet positions, arm angle, and breathing control were carefully coached. Any flinching or trigger-jerking tendencies were diplomatically corrected.

Because of Jackie's strong interest and motivation, the first training session ran two hours at her insistence. That's two to four times longer than I'd recommend for sessions with a youngster or less-motivated adults. My wife is well coordinated, and her progress was rapid. Her peak score in that first session was eighty-seven out of a possible one hundred after about ninety minutes of practice. After that, muscle fatigue from the unfamiliar task of holding a handgun steady took its toll and her scores slumped ten to thirty points. To avoid any discouragement on her part, I explained that fatigue was working against her learning curve here.

Class two was air-rifle practice. Two were available: a scoped Crosman 177 CO_2 model, and a BSA 22 one-pump air rifle with open sights. To teach both scope and iron sights, both were used. Starting with a well-coached prone position, she was startled by how much easier a rifle holds on target compared to a handgun. That's one reason I started her with a pistol. With her confidence level up at the rifle session's outset, she soon produced practical hunting accuracy with either air gun.

An air rifle for training is handy, since it allows backyard (or even within-apartment) practice. Cheap shooting, too. But first check local or state ordinances on this. Although an earthen bank in the yard provided a safe backdrop, I still wanted a target backboard that would stop either 177 or 22 air-gun pellets. A warning here — ¼-inch plywood was easily penetrated at more than fifty feet with the BSA. We had to use ½-inch plywood. Beware of pellet bounce-back from any nontrap-metal plate.

For evening and bad weather shooting, a factory-made bullet trap with target holder was mounted in a basement fireplace. (A garage would be an alternative.) Just make sure there's enough light on the target. Now sitting and offhand (standing) positions were demonstrated and used. I bore down hard on these, since both are tougher to master than prone and are of much more value in hunting. Omitted was the kneeling position, rarely useful in the hunting field.

But start with prone. It's a quick confidence builder, and its steadiness allows concentration by the pupil on sight picture, breathing control, and trigger squeeze. Except in the high-cost competition models, most air rifles have poor triggers, and are frustrating to teach a beginner good trigger control. At least their scores should jump automatically when graduating to a rifle with a better trigger.

Finally came the time for shooting big-game rifles. Common sense dictated using milder calibers here, since the last thing I wanted to do was give her a built-in flinch problem. I know a lackbrain who thought it hilarious to let his petite wife fire her first shot with his hard-recoiling 375 H&H elk rifle. It did not give her a flinching habit only because she flatly refused to ever fire any rifle again. Except possibly at him.

One useful tip here. If the only rifle available is something like a stiff-recoiling 30–06, obtain 22 Accelerator factory loads with sabot bullets for 06 use. Thanks to the very light bullets, these have negligible recoil and are fun to shoot.

Author's wife Jackie, taking practice shots from the sitting position, learned part of her basics with a BSA air rifle before moving to a bigger rifle. Author finds that women seem to learn marksmanship faster than men *if* not punished by muzzle blast and excessive recoil.

My wife's big-rifle debut included hearing protectors and a little recoil padding. True, no one seems to notice recoil when shooting at game, but beginners certainly do firing at targets. Thanks to mastering the basics with plenty of air rifle shooting, she was confident. Her skill surpassed my expectations. I've taught several girls and women to shoot. In my opinion, females pick up rifle marksmanship with ease *if* not punished by blast and recoil. Marksmanship is basically hand-eye coordination, something women probably excel at. (You question that? Try matching your womenfolk in threading a needle.)

Soon it was time to start thinking about a rifle of her own. Four "musts" were self evident: First, a reasonably mild-recoil caliber — common sense with any beginner, sex notwithstanding; second, a fairly flat trajectory for longer western shots; third, a power practical for elk, too (requiring some compromising with recoil); fourth, a rifle-scope combo not tiresomely heavy to pack around. She particularly enjoyed shooting a Savage 99 lever gun of mine in 284 cal. This rifle and load (approximating the popular 270) nicely fits all four requirements. (Other calibers meeting all four include the 270, 7x57, 7mm–08, 280 Remington, and 308. If the agenda lacks elk, the Savage 250, 257 Remington, and the 6-mm rounds are fine for deer.)

I shortened the buttstock about 1.5 inches. This was based on trigger-pull measurements taken when she was wearing hunting clothes. This also was a convenient time to refinish the stock, which had lots of saddle-scabbard wear. Finally, a formal presentation complete with applause and huzzas from other family hunters. A little ceremony here is like chicken soup for invalids — it might help and sure can't hurt. It is now *her* rifle, and if I want to use it, I ask her permission. Incidentally, Jackie's first shot at a mule deer resulted in a hit at 225 paces, a range I've seen quite a few male hunters miss at, not to mention a few misses of my own.

If doubtful of your qualifications to play firearms instructor even within your own family, help is available. The National Rifle Association, 1600 Rhode Island Ave. NW, Washington DC 20036, is the fountainhead of shooting sports training materials. Most states by now require training courses for juvenile hunters and presumably offer on-request gun training and safety material. Try your game department. Most libraries have books on basic firearms marksmanship.

Of course, there's far more to hunting than just guns and shooting. My new hunting partner's next training was in woodcraft, wildlife, and camping. Since I rarely hunt from a cabin or motel, the opening agenda was to do some backcountry-familiarization camping before hunting seasons. These trial runs were useful to field test new equipment in the process of upgrading camp gear. For starters, make sure the lady has *warm* bedding. Physiologically, women don't seem to have the tolerance to cold that men do. Not that I see any great karma in my own teeth chattering, either. Some overdue additions were made to cooking gear, too. Basic compass and map reading were taught in the course of this along with general information on whatever game we planned to hunt. We had a good season later, taking two mulies, a pronghorn, and a worthwhile elk. The lady enjoyed herself. I enjoyed her pleasure.

*   *   *

If teaching my wife went well, it was in part due to experience years earlier involving the boys. My biggest mistake there was not realizing that daughters may want to be hunters, too. Many years later, a now-grown oldest daughter told me how she secretly yearned to be invited by me and her brothers. Had I only known! It was too late when I found this out after she was married, tied down with small children, and living elsewhere in the bargain. I did manage to make up lost ground with another daughter, she who eventually brought a new husband into the hunting party as cited earlier.

Most states have a minimum age, usually twelve to fourteen, for youngsters to hunt big game and then usually only after passing a state-run firearms-safety course. However, the child's outdoor education can start well before that. Kick it off with enjoyable events: nonhunting hikes, overnight camping under easy conditions. My father, bless him, took me on my first hunting campout at age three. Maybe that was a tad early, but it certainly didn't turn me off hunting.

A sportsman's child has its first experience with hunting when dad brings home game. This means dead animals. The young child oftens questions this lack-of-life phenomenon. Level with the child that the game, be it deer or whatever, is dead in order to make food for the family table. The legitimate comparison (lost on the antihunters) is that animals are also killed in order to provide hamburgers at McDonald's or the leather in our shoes. This is reality, not morbidity. In the rare case that the child is turned off or revolted by the death factor in hunting, don't press the issue. Continue to treat it lightly as a routine nonissue like the super-market meat in the weekly groceries.

As the child gets older, hunting stories and good natural history books are useful educational devices. Today's TV fare alternately helps and hurts here. Sometimes wildlife programs accurately show the world of nature as (by our standards) a ruthless realm where all living things sooner or later die—many of them by the routine violence of the eaters-and-eaten natural food chain. By our ethics, most of those "natural"

deaths are terrible — the still-living, hamstrung deer torn and leisurely
eaten by timber wolves. Or the oversized deer herd decimated by starvation, which is nature's *routine* population control, not a rare abnormality.
To my children, I'd then comment that for us to eat venison too was just
as "natural," only our quick bullets are more humane. (Not that the wolf
is "bad.") And isn't it easier on the deer *and* their habitat to thin a herd by
hunting rather than by starvation? But hooked on half-truth, TV never
mentions this side of the coin.

Much TV is ecological claptrap. Remember that prime-time show
about a frontier recluse, his pet grizzly bear, and their marvelously non-
violent relationship with all other creatures? The vague impression was
that the buckskin philosopher and his half-ton omnivore lived on air and
grass. The original Grizzly Adams, whom this show caricatured, and his
grizzlies were meat eaters in the natural fashion of grizzly *and* man. This
record was firmly set straight for my kids. The show as presented was as
much fantasy as an animated cartoon.

During natural history programs, it's also good medicine to point
out to your troops that the main support for wildlife protection and
enhancement comes from hunters (sports fishermen too). Never yet have I
heard this on a television wildlife show. Historically we hunters have been
the only ones who really care enough about wildlife to pony up the hard
cash to protect and perpetuate those resources. A few years ago, it came
to light how one of the antihunting "save wildlife" private foundations
was *really* spending its money. Its only tangible project had been to
establish a cat-spaying clinic in Manhattan. The rest of its income from
well-meaning citizens and give-away foundations (who can be the world's
biggest suckers) went for administrative overhead. Translated, that means
comfortable salaries and expense accounts for the smart folks who
founded and run this charade. Perfectly legal, of course.

*   *   *

Start firearms safety training very early with youngsters. Short of a
Diebold bank vault on the premises, there's no completely foolproof way
to isolate household guns from inquisitive post-toddler children. Instead,
the child must be carefully and seriously taught that guns are potentially
dangerous, never to be examined without parental supervision. My dad
was good at this and enough of a practical psychologist to back it up by
letting me see, handle, and help clean his guns under his supervision.
Giving the child a piece of the action this way makes him a party to the
ruling safety code and thus likelier to observe it. Don't depend on locked

gun cabinets. Kids can be junior Houdinis in making naught of locks, simply because they're untiring in finding the inevitable hidden key.

Begin with carefully supervised airgun or 22 rimfire rifle practice. How early depends on the individual child. With some, eight years old is not too soon. Size-related ability to shoulder even a short-stocked weapon is a key factor. With a youngster, I would not start with a handgun. This should be formal training — hard and fast safety rules in no uncertain terms and close supervision at every step. Do not treat it casually.

With youngsters, discouragement can be an early problem. Training tips in breathing control and trigger squeeze are essential. Again, start with dry firing before real shooting is done. The beginner must be made to understand that he/she is not a failure because the bull's-eye or even entire target sheet was missed. To build confidence, start with easy close-range shooting. Use paper targets to encourage precision. Busting bottles and cans teaches imprecise shooting already in oversupply in the hunting field. Rifle marksmanship is learned fastest with a scope due to the simplicity of a crosshair sight picture.

Most states set age twelve as the big-game hunting threshold, and many require completion of the state-sponsored firearms course. If your youngster has already been trained at home, make sure he or she takes the required course in good grace with open ears nonetheless. Extra training won't hurt.

Choosing a youngster's big-game rifle should follow the same guidelines as in picking one for a wife or girlfriend. Don't overgun. Accurate shot placement should never be traded for excess power. A shortened stock might be needed.

But before that time, find out how interested the youngster really is in hunting. Some simply are not, and their reasons can vary. Although not a child psychologist, I think it would be disastrous to treat a child's indifference to hunting with you as a character defect on the kid's part. Of my three sons, one developed into a hunter more ardent and skilled than I am. Another likes hunting but doesn't bust his butt over it. The third quite calmly gave it up at a fairly early age despite shooting well and nicely getting a deer in his first season. Mechanically gifted, he decided rebuilding cars was more interesting and didn't require predawn reveille. He's a good man, and to date I haven't thought of a rational rebuttal defending hunting's admittedly atrocious starting hours.

Sometimes a beginning hunter's age is irrelevant. The daughter earlier cited didn't get into hunting until her middle twenties, but then went all out. She loves still-hunting on her own in far-back timber, outshoots most men at preseason target ranges, and is proud of her two big-game rifles — one of which she bought herself.

Common sense dictates that beginners shouldn't be exposed to unusually tough hunting. To this day my wife dislikes chukar partridge hunting because her first (and last) chukar trip was exhausting in very hot weather and mean terrain. Also, be sure your family partners are properly equipped. Being chronically cold or wet will frostbite any enthusiasm in the bud. Bear in mind, too, that women, bless them, are often less immune to some of the natural grubbiness during life in the great and often grimy outdoors. If a hunting trip can be interrupted overnight for a hot shower in a motel or commercial campground, the lady's morale upsurge will surprise you both.

*   *   *

Last but not least. You have failed badly if you train a hunter without sportsmanship values. With my family, I've always stressed that to enjoy the hunting trip is the real objective, not how much game is taken — if any. Days with an empty bag are not regarded as failure. Instead the slogan is: "The hunting is *always* good! Sometimes the *getting* may be poor." Never use scorn or ridicule. That doesn't rule out thorough correction of bad safety habits or violations of hunting ethics. Just remember that you set the example — win, lose, or draw.

Good hunting buddies are among the best things this world offers. They're all the better when they're a product of your teaching and example. The biggest thrill of all is when your family-member pupil excels you in smart hunting tactics, woodcraft, or shooting. After all, look who trained 'em!

15

Heading Off
Hunting Dangers

The outdoors is safer than much of modern society (try big cities after dark). But it's still a place where we can get into three different categories of trouble involving: 1) terrain and weather; 2) other creatures, ranging from bugs to bears; and 3) our own various ineptitudes.

Steep country always requires caution. One friend of mine took a twenty-five-foot fall while mountain hunting. A year later he's still undergoing spinal rehabilitation and is lucky not to be paralyzed, says his doctor. Avoid areas that require travel on all fours. If you must cross such a spot, keep your weight on your feet for maximum stability. Use hands only for supplementary support. Do not use knees and elbows. Move only one limb at a time. Where possible, kick dirt to make foot and handholds.

Never crawl inverted downhill with your back to a slope as if you were going to slide down it — just what you're likely to do, out of control. Face into the hill instead. When sidehilling, walk erect. Leaning into the sidehill is more tiring and offers less secure footing. A common danger is to start down a slope, then get down to where you find it impossibly dangerous to continue. But you may find it much more dangerous to climb back up than it was to lower yourself down that far. Lesson: Never start descending a steep grade that you cannot first evaluate for safety.

To conserve strength, use the alpine climber's trick of the uphill "rest step." Your heart actually spends more time resting than working. You can do this with your legs. Each time you move one leg uphill, pause momentarily with your weight resting on the downhill leg. This gives the uphill leg muscles a short but useful rest. You'll need fewer trailside rest stops.

Acute mountain sickness, or AMS, can be a serious affliction above eight thousand feet, and mountain hunters are often well above that. Symptoms are: 1) severe, constant headache *not* relieved by aspirin; 2) lack of balance and coordination; 3) tiring easily; 4) sense of helplessness and lack of purpose; 5) breathlessness and weakness; 6) pale or bluish skin color; 7) persistent, moist coughing; 8) insomnia and lack of appetite. Anyone with AMS symptoms should be promptly evacuated to below eight thousand feet. AMS holds risk of brain or lung edema (fluid buildup), a too-common cause of death among alpine climbers. Just the equilibrium-loss symptom endangers anyone hiking or horseback riding in rough country. For lowlanders, taking a couple extra days in lesser elevations to acclimatize to higher country is helpful in preventing AMS. So is good prehunt physical conditioning.

Avalanches can be a hazard, particularly in autumn when accumulations of unstable wet snow occur in sudden storms. Post-storm warming trends can destabilize new snow very quickly. Ask Colorado hunter Don Shake. He was swept away and buried by an avalanche in the Rockies and was lucky enough to be dug out alive, although injured. Or ask Washington snowshoers Ronald and Duncan Thomson who were buried but survived, albeit with a broken arm and leg between them. Foot pressure or noise (even a rifle shot?) can set avalanches off.

Even a shallow knee-deep avalanche is dangerous, since it irresistibly sweeps a person off his feet. My son was the only one of a hiking party not to be swept away by a Cascades snow slide of that kind. All luckily survived. But casualties often occur when victims are smashed into trees or rocks by the 60 to 70 mph giant hand of the avalanche (they've been clocked at 200 mph). In slab-type avalanches, people have been entombed when buried only six inches deep because the snow can compress like concrete.

Avoid hiking across or under typical avalanche slopes with sharply convex or concave surfaces holding a buildup of snow. The run-out zone

Autumnal storms usually produce wet, unstable snow that tends to form avalanches. Terrain need not be especially steep to generate snow slides. Slab avalanches like this one can entomb a human helplessly under only six inches of extremely compressed snow. — *U.S. Forest Service Photo*

of an avalanche can be far below where the slide starts. Leeward slopes (usually facing east-southeast-south) are the likeliest to avalanche. Old slide paths (see Chapter 9) are easily spotted with their long-bent and broken trees and brush — proof that vegetation can't be depended on to stop sizable slides.

Material on avalanches is available from U.S. Forest Service regional offices in the mountain states. (A chilling historical footnote: in World War I, Austrian and Italian troops fighting in the Alps lost over forty thousand men in snowslides, according to *The Avalanche Enigma,* by Fraser Colin, one of several books on the white killer.)

Camp sites can be hazardous. Avoid old timber where dead branches or whole trees can fall, with or without wind. One person was killed that way in a Washington campground, closed afterward due to the highly dangerous old timber (that diehard environmentalists wouldn't hear of logging). Camping on the conveniently level floodplain along western rivers or even dry watercourses is notoriously risky. A few years back, dozens of lives, many of them campers, were lost in a flash flood along the Big Thompson River in Colorado, and streamside campers never had a chance in the terrible Rapid City storm-triggered flood that killed 236 in 1972. The speed with which mountain-fed western streams can rise is unbelievable. Dry arroyos in the Southwest probably are the most dangerous.

Lightning is not to be ignored by muley hunters who are vulnerable in the high, typically open country receiving the most strikes. You're fairly safe in even-height timber. Since your rifle is a conductor, park it some distance from you. In the open, never sit under a lone tree. Stay low and try to find some overhang protection. Being in a metal vehicle is safe, but that may not apply to a plastic camper/trailer.

Heavy snow is nothing to fool with. If you're in a remote area, get out fast. Tire chains, repair links, chain tighteners, and a decent shovel are vital for any snowstorm driving, particularly in high country where a skid can be fatal. About every three to four years, a big storm traps scores of western hunters. They always get out but leave some stranded vehicles to be stripped all winter by snowmobiling vandals.

Hypothermia starts when your body's core temperature drops only three degrees and induces uncontrollable shivering. Along with that comes some loss of physical and mental ability to do such things as make a fire or even try to find shelter. If core temperature drops more, speech is impaired, and the victim may become irrational—like one afflicted outdoorsman in the Cascades who actually had to be restrained from jumping off a cliff as the fastest way to get off a stormswept mountain. Further body-temperature drops start affecting heartbeat and breathing until death occurs.

The dangerous thing about hypothermia, already cited in Chapter 3, is that *it can occur in the fifty-degree-Fahrenheit range.* When the above symptoms occur, get the victim's clothes off and skin dried. Next, reclothe in warm garments or in a sleeping bag prewarmed by another person—the victim's own body can't warm it up at this stage. If the bag is big enough, medical experts recommend putting the victim into it unclothed along with another unclothed, nonhypothermic person to effect the quickest transfer of body heat. No jokes—hypothermia is a serious emergency and the two-in-a-bag system may be the only system in an outdoor camp. Lacking heated shelter, get the victim between two or three campfires for fast warming. If a fire is raked away after burning, the person can be parked on the hot earth briefly to soak up heat. Since his own reactions may be too slow, be careful not to burn him.

Hot, sugary drinks, or even heated water, help put heat back into his core. No alcohol—it's a depressant, exactly the wrong thing here. Don't try to make the patient travel until he's fully conscious. There's too much chance of a bad fall that could compound the problem.

If the hypothermia victim is unconscious, keep him in a prone position with head tilted back to assure open breathing passage. Run a finger in the mouth to be certain he isn't choking on his tongue. Treating an unconscious hypothermia sufferer is a profound medical problem. The faster the patient can be gotten safely to a hospital, the better.

Frostbite is always a cold weather risk outdoors. Unfortunately, most people treat it exactly the wrong way when numbing or telltale white or gray spots on nose, cheeks, chin, ears, or fingers give warning. Never rub the frostbite with anything, including snow. Heat gently by putting your hands on the area or immersing it in tepid (not hot) water until circulation is restored. Frostbite requires medical attention as soon as possible in case complications develop.

Sunstroke and heat exhaustion are so medically complex that doctors today are not in agreement on actual definitions. Even the old term "sunstroke" is suspect, I am told. Because of this lack of medical consensus, a lay author is wise not to comment on the subject. Ask your own physician for advice, or read your own choice of a family medical book concerning treatment. The physician I did consult about this said the important things are to drink plenty of fluids and not overexert in hot weather. Anyone in your hunting crew suffering from fainting, dizziness, or nausea in very hot weather should be taken to medical treatment promptly, because these signals indicate a life-threatening condition.

Pathogens in water, among the "other creatures" hazards, lack the drama of bears or snakes. But they're far more likely problems, headed by a little-known, but very real pest called *Giardia lamblia,* the most common intestinal parasite in the U.S. Spread by fecal pollution, it causes giardiasis, also known as beaver fever, lasting from a week to several months with severe diarrhea, cramps, bloating, fatigue, and weight loss. It ruined a week-long muley/elk hunt for me.

Six recent camping and survival books I checked failed to mention giardiasis. Worse, some stated that backcountry water can be made safe by adding a little chlorine bleach to it. *Wrong.* Chlorine kills some bacteria but doesn't faze nonbacterial *Giardia*. Outbreaks have occurred in chlorinated municipal water in much of the West, which is how I got it. Red Lodge, Montana, topped three hundred cases in 1980, for example.

Iodine tablets, available from camping suppliers or pharmacies, kill *Giardia* but taint water flavor. Alternative: Boil water for at least ten minutes. Boiled water's flat taste is improved by pouring it between containers to aerate it. Yet a third purifier is a camper-potable water filter. Outdoor writer Stuart Williams, who hunts all over the world, tells me he has used such a filter with good results (no sickness) even with the chronically dangerous water of Latin America. Remember to treat water not just for drinking but also for washing utensils and brushing your teeth.

Salmonella and hepatitis are two of several other water problems. For example, Washington state health researchers report: "It's a myth that fast-moving water is safe. No stream . . . is safe to drink from . . . Water polluted by feces from beavers or muskrats is just plain contaminated."

In a lot of the West, people not used to highly alkaline local water suffer severe diarrhea. Bring drinking water from home or buy it bottled. For decades, my never-fail diarrhea remedy has been blackberry brandy (although I happen to dislike most liquor). For me, this stuff stops the run on the bank faster and better than Kaopectate. This is a purely personal observation, not a recommendation.

Bears of any size or breed have always been unpredictable and potentially troublesome creatures. That can now also be said of game-department bureaucrats. The updated policy of federal and state wildlife bureaucracies is that anyone killing a grizzly is guilty until proven innocent. While the grizzly merits Endangered Species protection in many areas, the concept has been carried to illogical extremes in true American fashion. Never shoot a protected bear except in absolute, him-or-you self defense. And lots of luck proving it to the Inquisition.

Grizzlies have always been short-fused enigmas. In Montana's Glacier National Park, several campers have been attacked and killed by grizzlies. Menstruating women are particularly vulnerable. In areas near Yellowstone, a few attacks have involved grizzlies earlier live-trapped in the national park and chemically tranquilized for tagging and examination. This has raised speculation about whether such drugging may be causing some bruin brain damage.

Don't underestimate black bears (which in the West can be brown or cream colored). As a newsman, I covered the death story of a husky fisherman who was bear-killed and partially eaten—this in northeastern Minnesota at least one thousand miles from the nearest wild grizzly. This case probably was an accidental run-in with a sow and cub, typically a

Even though grizzlies have more reputation for aggressiveness, black bears like this camp visitor can be unpredictably bad actors. Bear problems usually involve camp-food marauders. — *Jackie Nelson Photo*

risky situation. But there are numerous confirmed cases of unprovoked black bears attacking children and adults.

The likeliest either-species bear problem for hunters is the classic camp marauder. Hot-fire incineration of food wastes reduces odiferous waste foods, but letting garbage just smolder on a fire spreads its odor to possibly attract visitors. Put empty food cans in tightly closed plastic garbage bags to reduce their broadcast odor, too. Unfortunately, game hanging in camp can be a major attraction, discussed in Chapter 16 on meat care. Avoid storing drawing cards such as bacon or fish inside your tent. If a bear wants your grub, better that he doesn't come into the tent for it, particularly if he's a grizzly.

Ways to scare off a dangerously aggressive bear often appear solemnly in print. But bears individually may be too unpredictable to rely on such things as making loud noises or talking to a threatening bear in a moderate voice. It may work with Bear A but incite attack from Bear B.

Rattlesnake-encounter chances are overrated by many western hunters. That's not to say the snakes should be discounted—even if a statistical argument can be made that your home stairs and stepladder are 380 times more life threatening than a rattlesnake. Most hunters mistake harmless bullsnakes for rattlers. That multiplies their personal experience of "rattlers" seen, since bullsnakes are fairly common. Admittedly, there are hotspots like the Texas brush country where, I am assured by hunting chum Dave Petzal of *Field & Stream* magazine, *all* hunters wear snake-proof metal-mesh leggings. But let's look at some interesting statistics.

One, less than five percent of U.S. snakebite victims die. That's about fifty a year (compared to nineteen thousand deaths from home falls). Two, one medical survey showed that fifty percent of snakebite victims were apparently intoxicated at the time. Three, about seventy-five percent of bites are to hands and fingers, oddly enough, instead of the logically more vulnerable legs and ankles. Most interesting of all, forty percent of snakebite victims have tattoos. Are we looking at a personality profile of macho/impulsive types who deliberately mess around with snakes to show off to pals? Deducting these just-plain-asking-for-it cases drastically reduces the number of snakebites rating as genuine accidents.

But it does happen. The 12-year-old daughter of a rancher I know was struck on the finger by an unseen baby rattler in short lawn grass. She almost died, partly due to antivenin reaction. (Some research indicates that immature rattler venom may be five times more potent than that of mature snakes. Of the only three rattlers I've encountered while on foot, the most worrisome one was a seven-inch pencil-thick baby prairie rattler, because it was almost invisible even in very skimpy grass where I'd just been sitting when varmint shooting.)

Years ago I read the harrowing story of a deer hunter in Wyoming who sat on a flat rock. Without warning, he was struck in the leg by a rattler. The fangs caught in trouser cloth, holding the snake in place for more envenomation. The victim, a Wisconsin M.D., nearly died later in a hospital. Montanan Bill Shoup flopped forward over a rock to shoot an antelope. A big timber rattler, which Bill admits must have been in plain view, almost struck him right in the face. The attending physician told me of a hiker climbing rocks who reached up on a ledge and was struck in the hand. In these three snake-strike cases, there was no warning rattle. A southern doctor said that eighty-four of his snakebite patients never heard the snake rattle.

In snake country, program yourself to always look before you sit down, step over rocks or logs, or reach up on a ledge. Make this a habit like looking for traffic before you cross an intersection. Two areas deserve special caution. In autumn, rattlers seek rocky denning sites. Hot weather often finds them near water.

Treatment of snakebite is another area of medical disagreement. The pack-in-ice theory seems to be out the window. Even the longstanding X-cut over the fang marks and then sucking out the venom is suspect. One Texas doctor, after treating 118 snakebite cases, says that time is a greater enemy than exercise. So don't hesitate if you must hike out a couple miles to get medical help. Whatever the reason, in twenty-five percent of his snakebite victims, no venom was injected. The same practitioner reported no cases of strikes—even those of the big Texas diamondback—penetrating leather boots, if that cheers you up.

Poisonous insects kill ten times more Americans annually than snakebite, often people hypersensitive to bee, wasp, and hornet venom. If you're one of these, special treatment kits to have on hand can be obtained on prescription.

But anyone suffers highly toxic reaction to stings from scorpions or black widow spider bites, even though deaths are rare. The black widow has a distinctive red hourglass on its black body. The bite is described as a sharp pinprick followed by dull, numbing pain. Severe muscle spasms in the chest and abdomen may resemble appendicitis or heart attack. A victim's flushed face and spasm-induced grimaces are so typical that medics have a term for it: *Facies latrodectus,* or black widow face. Prompt medical attention is vital. One chap I know of got a black widow bite in California backcountry and wound up packed in ice and on a heart monitor in a hospital's intensive care unit. The young and old and those with heart disease or high blood pressure are likely to be most affected.

In scorpion country, check empty boots and bedding for these secretive menaces. A good black widow defense is wearing gloves when working on wood or brushpiles. In warm weather, I periodically give my tent floor a shot of aerosol bug killer. Against the threat of yellow jackets swarming around camp at mealtime, suspend a small piece of raw meat over a dish of water. Overfed yellow jackets fall off and drown. It really works.

Getting lost probably heads the self-inflicted-trouble category. This falls into two categories. One is not knowing exactly where you are but knowing which way is "out." By contrast, you are *really* lost when not knowing how to find your way out of wherever you are. This is totally preventable. Take a compass reading of your inbound direction. To get out, go in the opposite direction. Surprisingly, some hunters hit the woods without understanding that. More compass/map information appears in Chapter 2, but just following these simple steps makes it fairly difficult to get lost.

Don't think it takes being in the forest primeval to get lost. Without a compass, you can get disoriented in unfamiliar open country on overcast days without sun. A good argument can be made for a buddy system in hunting *and* for someone back home knowing where you're hunting and about when you're supposed to be back.

I maintain that in mountain country it's almost impossible to stay lost if you're able to travel. Normally, from high ground you can eyeball the landscape. Pick out an obvious valley (as differentiated from a no-exit basin), then go downhill into that. Except in true wilderness areas, you're almost sure to hit a road in this valley or the next one it feeds into. Even in the big national forests, there are plenty of roads. Once on a road, you are no longer really lost. You may not know where you are, but taking a road downgrade will bring you out somewhere. All roads have at least one end connecting to other roads.

Staying put until someone comes along your road is an option whose wisdom depends on weather, what kind of shape you're in, and how much use you realistically expect this road gets. If movement is possible, I'd vote not to wait for someone to show up. In many areas, backcountry roads are being closed off to reduce hunting pressure, and you could wind up squatting on one of those no-travel roads. *Don't* leave the darned road once you find one! One lost hunter I helped search for did just that and managed to stay lost many hours longer.

Never try to travel after dark. I had to do it once, but never again. Even in flat terrain, it's simply too dangerous unless you have a sizable flashlight. You only have to trip and fall a couple of feet to break an ankle for some serious trouble. In steep country, after-dark travel can be suicidal. If you have to siwash-camp it overnight, I hope you have a survival kit — *with you,* not sitting back at camp. Survival kits are exhaustively written about. Some include enough items and emergency food to founder anyone but a Sherpa porter. If lost, your big need will be for shelter and warmth. Lack of those could kill you overnight in bad weather, but you can go days without food. Water, of course, is the biggest problem in dry country. Much better is the minimum kit that I hope you'll discipline yourself to carry in daypack or game pocket at all times. Mine includes a light plastic tarp big enough to rig an open-faced reflective heat shelter in front of a fire. Tube tents sold for survival don't permit a fire. My kit also has energy-providing candy bars of a kind I dislike, and thus won't munch as nonemergency snacks.

The kit contains lots of big strike-anywhere matches in two (should one get lost) waterproof containers. Paraffin fire starters are important in wet weather. Also in the kit is a tightly packed down vest. These items are waterproof, packed in a heavy-duty plastic lawn bag which, with head and arm holes cut, makes a rain/snow garment. Included is about twenty feet of nylon cord to rig the shelter with enough left over to drag bundles of firewood—the quickest energy-saving way to stockpile fuel. For all-nighting it in cold weather, figure on laying in about twice as much firewood as you think you'll need. This *must* be done in daylight, since it's too difficult and risky to gather enough wood after dark.

Keeping a grip on yourself if lost is vital. Some people panic. An old forester told me of his search party finding a lost Indian-teenager deer hunter who'd literally run himself to death—stripping himself to the waist in bitter weather in the process. Some give up. One lost hunter was found where he'd spent many days, only four hundred yards of easy, downhill walking away from a mainstem logging road that had trucks going back and forth every twenty minutes, eight hours a day. He heard them but, although not disabled, had given himself up to die—and almost did.

To prevent disabling and potentially fatal falls, never hike in the dark without a good flashlight.

By contrast, a middleaged woman some thirty-plus years ago survived about a month in the Big Horns' high, cold environment after a plane crash that killed her husband. Although there was limited water nearby, she had almost no food and only the wrecked plane for shelter. The only thing she really had was a will to live—the most important "survival gear" of all.

Cutlery safety primarily covers chainsaws and axes. Both are dangerous, and never forget that when using them. Chainsaws make terrible wounds, says my M.D. hunting partner. Don't use one when you're fatigued. Once, one of our hunting party, very tired at the time, made a slip and cut through his trousers *and* long underwear without cutting the leg underneath, which is about as close as you can come. Be particularly leery about holding down a log with a foot and buzzing next to it with the saw. Chainsaw dealers and county extension service offices all offer good how-to literature on wise, safe chainsaw use.

Proper axe handling deserves more space than available here. Instead, get a book devoted solely to camping and woodcraft. In short: 1) dull axes are dangerous; 2) all hatchets are dangerous, because of easy deflection; 3) never split kindling by holding it with one hand and whacking it vertically with an axe. Instead, rest the horizontal piece firmly on good support, hold the end closest to you with one hand, and whack the other end (with the wood grain, or course) to get the axe imbedded. Then you can swing the wood ninety degrees and proceed to split vertically with both hands on the axe. There's no need to risk fingers hanging onto the wood.

Firearms safety is very simple—make sure you have muzzle control at all times. Genuine "stray bullet" accidents are rare. All studies show that if someone shoots you, chances are overwhelming it will be a partner, usually at very close range (typically when loading/unloading). So pick hunting partners with care—don't hunt with dingbats. Unload before climbing up or down trees or steep rocks. *Never* carry a loaded weapon in a vehicle—a common violation in the West where most states don't require cased rifles, tempting El Stupidos to keep a round chambered for road hunting. Don't accidentally use the wrong ammo; a buddy of mine fired a 270 cartridge in the oversized chamber of a 300 Weatherby with awesome gas-escape results. Monitor a beginner's gun handling closely.

Fires and fuels cover a multitude of potential safety sins. First, understand that wood is a dangerous fuel, not just in the standard risks of cutting and splitting it, but because it doesn't lend itself to as much control as hydrocarbon fuels. A while back, one of my buddies lost his neat mountain hunting cabin to an untended-wood-stove conflagration. Since then, a partner and I came very close to burning down our tent camp with too hot a wood stove one cold morning. Moral: Keep an extinguisher in your camp.

But LP bottle gas and gasoline require caution, too. Never refuel a gasoline lantern until it's been shut off several minutes to make sure the mantle isn't glowing. With gas stoves, always remove the tank for refueling. Store spare gasoline some distance from tent and fires. Make sure an LP cylinder is tightly in place. Due to a connection-seal leak, I once had a lantern of the unthreaded slip-in-gas-cartridge type burst into a fierce fire that nearly torched me and my travel trailer.

Never use open-flame devices for heating confined areas any length of time without ventilation. Asphyxiation from either monoxide or simple depletion of oxygen in a tightly closed camper kills a dismaying number of hunters — five in one camper a while back.

First aid training is worthwhile for outdoors recreationists who are often far from professional medical help. Just knowing how to use a tourniquet can be vital — would you believe sometimes these are misapplied below the wound? In addition to periodically offering courses, local Red Cross offices mail useful first-aid information on request, and it's a stock book item in any library.

In vehicle or camp, keep a first-aid kit for minor mishaps. Add to it: 1) a tube of butesyn picrate, the quickest pain-killing burn ointment; 2) a sharp needle and tweezers for sliver removal; 3) oil of cloves for an untoward toothache.

In summary — Yes, there is trouble potential in the great outdoors anytime. But most of it is of the self-induced variety. Very little of it will hit you unawares or unannounced. To repeat, that's more than you can say of some of the hazards of modern "civilized" society.

16

After Your Game
Is on the Ground

Rule No. 1: Never approach a fallen deer from the front. If it suddenly scrambles up and forward, the last place you want to be is ahead of those antlers propelled by two hundred pounds of panicky, powerful animal. (I had one almost get away when it recovered violently after a TKO from a 243 bullet hitting an antler.) Prod the animal in the back of the head or neck with the rifle muzzle. Watch for any breathing. To avoid damaging the cape for mounting, any final shot should go behind the shoulder—there is no important meat there. Otherwise shoot it in the neck behind the head. Don't attempt to dispatch a deer with a knife, since even a wounded muley buck may react with strength and speed. Next, do whatever the law requires about punching your tag. Many hunters honestly forget this and get into legal trouble.

Ignore the scent glands in the legs. Since that potent stuff can't reach edible portions unassisted, it makes no sense to get the knife smeared with that scent, then transmit it inside the animal in the field-dressing process. Outdoor writer Joe DeFalco, both an ardent deer hunter *and* a professional butcher, agrees.

Here is the basic field-dressing system. First, don't cut or slash the throat. That only ruins the neck for mounting and adds another entrance for dirt when dragging. Complete bleeding out will occur soon. Position the carcass, preferably lower at the rear, where you can work on it easily. Cut around the anus as you would core an apple. A slender, *sharp* hunting knife is best here. Probe the cut deeper with your fingers to continue separating the anus from adjoining tissue.

Working carefully to avoid going through the abdominal muscles, get the penis skinned loose but still intact to where it enters the pelvic structure. The testicles can be removed any time. (Yes, they are good eating — sliced and fried, they look and taste like scallops. No, my medical hunting partner says they won't do a thing for your savoir faire.)

I prefer to unzip the abdomen from between the hindquarters up to the rib cage. Carefully start a shallow cut through hide only. Skin back a couple inches of hide on both sides of this long incision to help keep hair out of the interior later. To cut through the muscle wall, turn your knife so the sharp side is upward, and use it at a 45-degree angle to slice with just the tip toward the front of the animal. With your other hand, insert two fingers slightly apart into the cut to depress the intestines and stomach below the knife tip. If you do this right, you'll have that knife tip between your depressor fingers, so be careful.

Pull out intestines and stomach. Cutting will be necessary to free this mass. If you did the job right on the anus, it will come out right along with the lower intestine, but do this part carefully to prevent feces from popping out.

Cut out the diaphragm, separating stomach from lungs. Working carefully, reach inside to cut loose lung tissue and heart. This is a bit easier if you have a meat saw to open the rib cage far up toward the neck (a good way to break a knife). If the animal has to be dragged some distance, I prefer not to open it up to entry of dirt or twigs any more than necessary.

To me, the trickiest part is getting the penis and attached bladder removed in one piece. First check your game regs to see if male organs must be left attached for legal sex identification. If you know where to cut — impossible to describe only in print, so use your eyes — the plumbing can be freed to come out the channel between the hams already enlarged by removal of the preseparated anus. Work carefully to avoid puncturing the bladder. Some hunters tie it off to prevent leakage if it tears loose from the penis. If you want heart and liver, separate them from the other innards. Next, turn the animal over, front end elevated, to drain blood from the body cavity.

Controversial is the use of water or snow to clean the cavity. Some claim that water invites spoilage. But it's essential to clean digestive juices out of a paunch-shot animal. In the arid West, I have routinely sluiced scores of deer with water to clean out blood. Never have I had a carcass go bad from this moisture. I do make sure that the cavity gets gravity drained and wiped dry. Professional butcher DeFalco is another water user, adding salt to it — a good idea, since salt has some germicidal value. If weather is mild and downright moist, I *don't* use water, due to too-slow drying and spoilage risk, and only dry-wipe the blood out.

*   *   *

What comes next depends on how you'll transport the game. If man-dragging it to a vehicle, hook the front legs up over the antlers to facilitate dragging. With some commonsense rope work, you can tie the drag line to the front feet and antlers this way to avoid chafing the hide around the neck if it's to be mounted.

If dragging the carcass behind a horse, remove the lower legs to avoid catching them in brush. A horse is too dumb to stop and strong enough to keep pulling hard with possibly dire results. Take off lower legs by cutting around the knee joints, through cartilage, and wrench them off — no sawing needed. Make sure not to cut the rear tendons above the joint, since they're useful for hanging carcass or quarters.

An urgent warning. When horse-dragging a deer, *do not tie the rope to your saddle horn*. This is known as the hospital hitch. If the tightly tied deer slides off a trail downhill or hangs up hard, that taut rope will knock you right out of the saddle if it doesn't first darned near saw you in half. (I made that mistake just once and had a bad back for six months.) Instead, just take a couple of dallies (turns) of the drag rope around the saddle horn, allowing it to slip loose pronto if anything goes haywire — as things often do any time horses are involved, it seems.

To carry over a horse, the deer's lower legs must come off. Make a "button hole" in the belly flap hide near the gut opening to slip over the saddle horn to help hold the carcass in place. Along with lashing the carcass so it doesn't fall, securing the head is vital to keep antlers from gouging the horse.

Spooked by blood smell, horses often object to carrying game. The old guides' tricks are to blindfold the horse or smear a palmful of game blood over its nose. As the late Jack O'Connor said, then the whole world stinks, so the horse quits worrying about it. Although no good in open country, the only way I know for a non-weight-lifter to get a big buck up on a horse unassisted is to first hang up the deer. Use the horse for hoisting power. Halter-tie the horse where you can swing the hanging deer down on its back.

*   *   *

In some states, heart attacks when dragging deer kill about as many big-game hunters as gunshot mishaps. Don't drag it alone unless the distance is short and the going easy. The best way is to find a stout pole to use as a cross-midriff "tow bar" supported in the crook of both elbows. The drag rope forms a V from the ends of the stick back to the front of the deer, triced up as cited above for easy pulling. This works even better with two people dragging, assuming a longer tow bar. If only the gut cavity has been opened, little or no dirt will enter. Snow, of course, means easy dragging.

Easiest way to drag a downed deer is with this "tow-bar" arrangement. A single hunter can position himself between the double lines connected to the deer. Deer's front legs are tied to antlers to facilitate dragging.

Dangerous on broken ground and misery on any ground is the two-man carry of a deer slung from a pole. Backpacking is better, but the deer must be skinned, then taken apart. For the latter, use the flesh side of the hide as a working surface to help keep meat clean. It's a great idea to have some cheesecloth game bags for quarters or boned-out meat. To halve or quarter requires a small meat saw, far better than a hatchet and lighter to carry in your pack. Careful boning following natural muscle separations as much as possible can be done without saw splitting the carcass, but it takes some time. A man in reasonable shape can handle half a mule deer on a packboard or practically all of it if boned out (about seventy pounds, not counting hide and head). On a steep climb, take rests and use a hiking staff. Put some blaze orange marking tape or cloth on an antlered head on a packboard.

If it is necessary to leave the kill awhile, don't skin and quarter it, since the exposed meat is too vulnerable to blowflies and birds. First get the carcass off the ground for better cooling. Placing it gut-cavity down over a sage clump or rock makes it harder for magpies, the pest of the West, to get at the meat. I unwisely left a nice dressed-out buck on its back to speed cooling while I hiked for help. When we came back in less than an hour, magpies had eaten the inner loins and much of the hams. Cheesecloth would keep them and the blowflies out. A network of branches will keep out crows and ravens who could make short work of cheesecloth.

A bird-scaring trick I just heard about is to hang an inflated paper sack swinging in the wind above or very near a deer carcass. Drawing big owl eyes on the sack may help, since magpies fear owls.

Coyotes? If there's no hoisting tree to get the deer out of their reach, urinate in two or three places near the carcass. So far, that's never failed me. Fearing traps, coyotes won't come near that man smell for days. Nothing will keep a hungry bear away. Hoisting the carcass well into a tree may foil a grizzly but not a black bear, who can out-shinny utility linemen. The normally shy mountain lion's nerve-fraying habit of discreetly trailing a hunter is probably because of experience-based hopes that sooner or later this human will provide a game-gut pile, something these big cats are quick to scavenge. Although I haven't lost a deer this way, my bet is that a lion is unlikely to pass up a deer carcass freebie, human scent notwithstanding.

Once the whole animal is out of the boondocks, it's best to skin promptly for quicker cooling, easier skinning, and to allow complete cutting out of bloodshot meat around bullet holes. Any spoilage will start there and rapidly spread into undamaged meat nearby. Although leaving the hide on helps keep meat dry when the hanging game is exposed to wet weather, rigging a rainproof tarp over it is better. Allow clearance for cooling air circulation. If you don't skin, cut open the neck and chest area as soon as possible for cooling and to remove the quick-souring windpipe and esophagus. Do that *after* trophy caping. Short sticks can wedge open the body opening for better cooling.

There are arguments both ways about hanging deer by head or hind legs. I vote for head down because: 1) it's easier to skin and saw-split the backbone when hung by the hocks; 2) no rope-rub damage occurs to the neck if you want it mounted; 3) the carcass cools quicker with the body cavity pointed up this way. Skin with a sharp knife with lots of curvature at the front — the opposite of a slender blade that is better for cleaning game. Depending on how far you skin down the legs, this is the time to get rid of the scent gland there. Work carefully to avoid hide cuts if you want tanned buckskin later. In warm weather, scrape the hide free of fat and meat scraps, heavily salt it, tightly roll, and tie it.

Due to cooling in the West's chilly nights, game can keep a few days if protected from sun's warmth. An old defense against blowflies is to rub lots of black pepper into the softer, moister meat areas. But a game bag is better if it has no fly-entrance gaps. To make sure, double up with two bags. Hanging game in a dark area, such as a no-window ranch outbuilding, stops blowflies because they're only active in light.

In author's experience, it's easy to keep trap-shy coyotes away from game carcasses if the hunter leaves plenty of man-scent by urinating nearby.

In transit, protect game from sun and engine heat. For a long trip home in mild weather, I like to hit the road early in the morning with the game cold from the night's chill. I cover (not wrap) it to stay cool, yet with some air circulation—for instance, I have a side window open in my pickup's canopy. In hot weather, an alternative is to make the trip at night. Hunters facing a long drive may be best off packing the meat in boxes with dry ice, obtainable in larger towns during hunting season. Since you don't want the meat frozen before final cutting and packaging, cover the game with a sleeping bag to keep it from freezing on a long haul in frigid weather.

Conversion of the carcass into actual eatin' meat is shown on the accompanying chart. You have some options, starting with converting the whole deer to ground meat and sausage, the time-honored method with an old buck presumed tough. With a few days of cool aging, even the older bucks tenderize, however. If in doubt, cut more for roasts than chops and steaks. Get rid of all fat—from deer, it tastes terrible—and bloodshot meat missed earlier. Wrap convenient amounts in good freezer paper and seal well against freezer burn. Some prefer to mix ground venison with ground pork for added fat. Pork flavor deteriorates after a few months in a freezer. Better to freeze ground venison alone, then mix with fresh ground pork at the time of use.

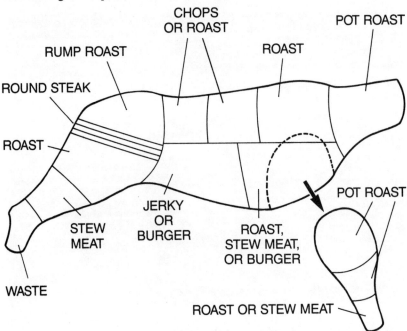

Good venison requires tender, loving care in cooking. Very lean, it's low in calories and cholesterol. It makes great jerky and chili. But over-cooked, it dries out with dramatic flavor loss. Some people think that venison has to be thoroughly cooked to avoid trichinosis, the muscle parasite possible in pork and common in bear. This is not true, and venison on the rare side beats venison cooked to resemble cardboard.

* * *

Caping or skinning out the neck and head of a buck is time-consuming and delicate. For a full-shoulder mount, cut the hide around the deer behind the shoulders. Then make a careful cut up the back line to a point almost between the ears. Forming a Y, run incisions to the base of each antler. From there on, an X-acto or similar hobby knife with sharp, spare blades helps in the tricky time-consuming skinning of eyelids, nose area, and lips. Unless a hunter has had previous coaching from his taxidermist, it's safest to remove the head with cape, and get it either into a freezer or to a taxidermist very shortly. Salting the cape offers no protection of the unskinned head, so don't dally in warm weather.

If you want only an antler mount, saw through the skull plate about on a level line, circumscribing it through the eyes and around the back of the head. Keep this line even all the way around. If in doubt, cut off more rather than less skull top. The sawing is much easier and more controllable if you take a few minutes to peel away hide where you plan to cut.

Some taxidermists buy extra capes, since customers often bring in badly butchered heads for mounting. Before selling a cape to a taxidermist, check your state's game laws. Some flatly forbid any sale of game or portions thereof.

* * *

Meat-care tools largely depend on how and where you're hunting. Obviously, a backpack hunter is limited in his hardware. The minimum outfit should include two knives: one a light, slender job for basic cleaning (a quality jacknife is fine), the other a good skinning knife. Include at least a pocket sharpening stone. If you have room, the modern ceramic "rabbit ears" sharpening system is easy and safe. Don't forget a meat saw.

Game bags and plenty of rope for hanging or packing game take little room and weight. A hunter's pulley hoist is dandy when neither equine nor mechanical horsepower are available to save hoisting efforts. (It is odd how hunters will sweat and swear to hoist game without thinking that a stout rope and their vehicle will do the job painlessly.) Rock salt

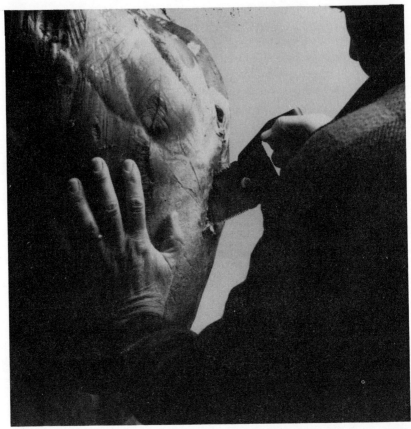

Excellent for sawing through the length of the spine is this Michaels of Oregon sportsmen's saw. It has meat-cutting teeth on one side of the blade and offset wood-cutting teeth on the other.

can be important in a warm-weather hunt. Waterless soap does a good job of cleaning tallow and dried blood from hands and arms.

One final note. Since they're often only familiar with packaged supermarket meat, seeing deer brought home and cut up makes many a good wife squeamish. But if you have a helpmeet who rolls up her sleeves, helps cut and package venison, and cooks it with consideration for its delicacy, keep that lady from catching cold or walking against red lights. You can't hardly get that kind no more.

17

Mule Deer Hunting – Here Today, Gone Tomorrow?

Mule deer are hardy wildlife, capable of adapting to a variety of conditions. They're very likely here to stay. The key questions are in what numbers and what quality. But mule deer hunters could be an endangered species unless we do some adapting of our own. Change is being thrust upon us. Some of it can cloud the future of mule deer hunting.

* * *

To some hunters, no muley is a trophy unless it "makes the book," meaning the antlers score highly enough in typical or nontypical categories to merit listing in the Boone and Crockett Club records. See the accompanying forms for further information on this, including scoring procedures. It might be easier statistically to go out and win a state lottery. Figure it out. Of the millions of mule deer taken, there are only a few hundred in Boone and Crockett.

Trophy listings, of themselves, indicate only some ritualized mathematical measurements. They prove nothing about the quality of the

OFFICIAL SCORING SYSTEM FOR NORTH AMERICAN BIG GAME TROPHIES

Records of North American
Big Game

BOONE AND CROCKETT CLUB

205 South Patrick Street
Alexandria, Virginia 22314

Minimum Score:
mule   195
blacktail 130

TYPICAL
MULE AND BLACKTAIL DEER

Kind of Deer _____

DETAIL OF POINT
MEASUREMENT

Abnormal Points	
Right	Left

Total to E

SEE OTHER SIDE FOR INSTRUCTIONS		R.	L.	Column 1 Spread Credit	Column 2 Right Antler	Column 3 Left Antler	Column 4 Difference
A.	Number of points on Each Antler						
B.	Tip to Tip Spread						
C.	Greatest Spread						
D.	Inside Spread of Main Beams	Credit may equal but not exceed length of longer antler					
IF Spread exceeds longer antler, enter difference							
E.	Total of Lengths of Abnormal Points						
F.	Length of Main Beam						
G-1. Length of First Point, if present							
G-2. Length of Second Point							
G-3. Length of Third Point, if present							
G-4. Length of Fourth Point, if present							
H-1. Circumference at Smallest Place Between Burr and First Point							
H-2. Circumference at Smallest Place Between First and Second Points							
H-3. Circumference at Smallest Place Between Main Beam and Third Point							
H-4. Circumference at Smallest Place Between Second and Fourth Points							
	TOTALS						

ADD	Column 1		Exact locality where killed
	Column 2		Date killed By whom killed
	Column 3		Present owner
	TOTAL		Address
SUBTRACT Column 4			Guide's Name and Address
FINAL SCORE			Remarks: (Mention any abnormalities or unique qualities)

(Front side of form)

I certify that I have measured the above trophy on _____ 19 _____
at (address) _____
                                          City   State _____
and that these measurements and data are, to the best of my knowledge and belief, made in accordance
with the instructions given.

Witness: _____ Signature: _____

OFFICIAL MEASURER [ ][ ][ ][ ]

INSTRUCTIONS FOR MEASURING MULE AND BLACKTAIL DEER

All measurements must be made with a ¼-inch flexible steel tape to the nearest one-eighth of an inch.
Wherever it is necessary to change direction of measurement, mark a control point and swing tape at
this point. Enter fractional figures in eighths, without reduction. Official measurements cannot
be taken for at least sixty days after the animal was killed.

A. Number of Points on Each Antler. To be counted a point, a projection must be at least one inch
long and its length must exceed the width of its base. All points are measured from tip of point to
nearest edge of beam as illustrated. Beam tip is counted as a point but not measured as a point.

B. Tip to Tip Spread is measured between tips of main beams.

C. Greatest Spread is measured between perpendiculars at a right angle to the center line of the
skull at widest part whether across main beams or points.

D. Inside Spread of Main Beams is measured at a right angle to the center line of the skull at widest point between main beams. Enter this measurement again in Spread Credit column if it is less
than or equal to the length of longer antler; if longer, enter longer antler length for Spread Credit.

E. Total Lengths of all Abnormal Points. Abnormal points are those nontypical in location such as
points originating from a point (exception: G-3 originates from G-2 in perfectly normal fashion) or
from sides or bottom of main beam or any points beyond the normal pattern of five (including beam
tip) per antler. Measure each abnormal point in usual manner and enter in appropriate blanks.

F. Length of Main Beam is measured from lowest outside edge of burr over outer curve to the tip of
the main beam. The point of beginning is that point on the burr where the center line along the
outer curve of the beam intersects the burr, then following generally the line of the illustration.

G-1-2-3-4. Length of Normal Points. Normal points are the brow and the upper and lower forks as
shown in the illustration. They are measured from nearest edge of beam over outer curve to tip.
Lay the tape along the outer curve of the beam so that the top edge of the tape coincides with the
top edge cf the beam on both sides of the point to determine baseline for point measurement. Record
point lengths in appropriate blanks.

H-1-2-3-4. Circumferences are taken as detailed for each measurement. If brow point is missing,
take H-1 and H-2 at smallest place between burr and G-2. If G-3 is missing, take H-3 halfway between
the base and tip of second point. If G-4 is missing, take H-4 halfway between the second point and
tip of main beam. * * * * * * * * * * * *

FAIR CHASE STATEMENT FOR ALL HUNTER-TAKEN TROPHIES

To make use of the following methods shall be deemed as UNFAIR CHASE and unsportsmanlike, and any
trophy obtained by use of such means is disqualified from entry for Awards.

   I. Spotting or herding game from the air, followed by landing in its vicinity
     for pursuit;
  II. Herding or pursuing game with motor-powered vehicles;
 III. Use of electronic communications for attracting, locating or observing
     game, or guiding the hunter to such game;
 IV. Hunting game confined by artificial barriers, including escape-proof fencing;
     or hunting game transplanted solely for the purpose of commercial shooting.
     ****

I certify that the trophy scored on this chart was not taken in UNFAIR CHASE as defined above by the
Boone and Crockett Club. I further certify that it was taken in full compliance with local game laws
of the state, province, or territory.
Date_____ Signature of Hunter_____
(Have signature notarized by a Notary Public)

(Reverse side of form)

Records of North American Big Game	BOONE AND CROCKETT CLUB	205 South Patrick Street Alexandria, Virginia 22314

Minimum Score: 240

NON-TYPICAL MULE DEER

Abnormal Points	
Right	Left
Total to E	

SEE OTHER SIDE FOR INSTRUCTIONS			Column 1	Column 2	Column 3	Column 4
	R.	L.	Spread Credit	Right Antler	Left Antler	Difference
A. Number of Points on Each Antler						
B. Tip to Tip Spread						
C. Greatest Spread						
D. Inside Spread of Main Beams — Credit may equal but not exceed length of longer antler						
IF Spread exceeds longer antler, enter difference						
E. Total of Lengths of Abnormal Points						
F. Length of Main Beams						
G-1. Length of First Point, if present						
G-2. Length of Second Point						
G-3. Length of Third Point, if present						
G-4. Length of Fourth Point, if present						
H-1. Circumference at Smallest Place Between Burr and First Point						
H-2. Circumference at Smallest Place Between First and Second Points						
H-3. Circumference at Smallest Place Between Main Beam and Third Point						
H-4. Circumference at Smallest Place Between Second and Fourth Points						
TOTALS						

ADD	Column 1		Exact locality where killed
	Column 2		Date killed By whom killed
	Column 3		Present Owner
	TOTAL		Address
SUBTRACT Column 4			
	Result		Guide's Name and Address
Add Line E Total			Remarks: (Mention any abnormalities or unique qualities)
FINAL SCORE			

(Front side of form)

I certify that I have measured the above trophy on _____ 19_____
at (address) _____ City _____ State_____
and that these measurements and data are, to the best of my knowledge and belief, made in accordance
with the instructions given.
Witness: _____ Signature: _____
                                                          OFFICIAL MEASURER | | | | |

INSTRUCTIONS FOR MEASURING NON-TYPICAL MULE DEER

All measurements must be made with a ¼-inch flexible steel tape to the nearest one-eighth of an inch.
Wherever it is necessary to change direction of measurement, mark a control point and swing tape at
this point. Enter fractional figures in eighths, without reduction. Official measurements cannot
be taken for at least sixty days after the animal was killed.

A. Number of Points on Each Antler. To be counted a point, a projection must be at least one inch
long and its length must exceed the width of its base. All points are measured from tip of point to
nearest edge of beam as illustrated. Beam tip is counted as a point but not measured as a point.

B. Tip to Tip Spread is measured between tips of main beams.

C. Greatest Spread is measured between perpendiculars at a right angle to the center line of the
skull at widest part whether across main beams or points.

D. Inside Spread of Main Beams is measured at a right angle to the center line of the skull at widest point between main beams. Enter this measurement again in Spread Credit column if it is less
than or equal to the length of longer antler; if longer, enter longer antler length for Spread Credit.

E. Total of Lengths of all Abnormal Points. Abnormal points are those nontypical in location or
points beyond the normal pattern of five (including beam tip) per antler. Mark the points that are
normal, as defined below. All other points are considered abnormal and are entered in appropriate
blanks, after measurement in usual manner.

F. Length of Main Beam is measured from lowest outside edge of burr over outer curve to the tip of
the main beam. The point of beginning is that point on the burr where the center line along the outer
curve of the beam intersects the burr, then following generally the line of the illustration.

G-1-2-3-4. Length of Normal Points. Normal points are the brow and the upper and lower forks, as
shown in the illustration. They are measured from nearest edge of beam over outer curve to tip. Lay
the tape along the outer curve of the beam so that the top edge of the tape coincides with the top
edge of the beam on both sides of the point to determine baseline for point measurement. Record
point lengths in appropriate blanks.

H-1-2-3-4. Circumferences are taken as detailed for each measurement. If brow point is missing,
take H-1 and H-2 at smallest place between burr and G-2. If G-3 is missing, take H-3 halfway between
the base and tip of second point. If G-4 is missing, take H-4 halfway between the second point and
tip of main beam. * * * * * * * * * * * *

FAIR CHASE STATEMENT FOR ALL HUNTER-TAKEN TROPHIES

To make use of the following methods shall be deemed as UNFAIR CHASE and unsportsmanlike and any
trophy obtained by use of such means is disqualified from entry for Awards.
    I.   Spotting or herding game from the air, followed by landing in its vicinity
         for pursuit;
   II.   Herding or pursuing game with motor-powered vehicles;
  III.   Use of electronic communications for attracting, locating or observing
         game, or guiding the hunter to such game;
   IV.   Hunting game confined by artificial barriers, including escape-proof fencing;
         or hunting game transplanted solely for the purpose of commercial shooting.
         *
I certify that the trophy scored on this chart was not taken in UNFAIR CHASE as defined above by the
Boone and Crockett Club. I further certify that it was taken in full compliance with local game laws
of the state, province, or territory.
Date_____ Signature of Hunter_____
(Have signature notarized by a Notary Public)

(Reverse side of form)

hunt — or hunter. A trophy listing or even just a big rack mounted on the wall may mean that the recorded hunter was very good — or very lucky — or may know little about hunting but could afford to be an armed tourist piggybacking on the hunting skills of the best guide money could buy. And let's hope the trophy wasn't bought behind a tavern from the local poaching ace who jacklighted it the night before in an alfalfa meadow. (Ask the chief warden of any big-game state how many problems they've had in recent years involving a rebirth of market hunting for saleable trophy-game heads.)

Webster's defines "trophy" as: ". . . Any memorial of victory or conquest; as, *trophies* of the chase." The hunter himself, not a tape measure, is the only valid judge of whether his trophy involved challenge, achievement, overcoming difficulties, or whatever, as a "memorial of victory or conquest." Often the conquest is more over the hunter himself than the game — forcing his tired body to climb one last ridge, or staying out another hour or two in weather miserably hot, cold, or wet. True, the big-racked muley trophies often demand such effort from the hunter. But so do some physically lesser deer at times. It can be argued that in terms of tough hunting, the rather scrawny, small-antlered Columbia blacktail is the most demanding big-game trophy in North America, thanks to the problems of hunting its junglelike environment, autumnally drenched in nonstop rains.

When I started hunting mule deer in the Golden Age of the 1950s, big, unwary muley bucks were often too-easy game to rate as memorable trophies, antler size notwithstanding. I recall passing up one of the biggest mule deer I ever saw for two completely selfish reasons. First, because it was early on the opening day, and I refused to end a year-anticipated hunt that quickly. Second, by pure accident I caught him in a duck soup situation that amounted to assassination, not sport, had I pulled the trigger. His antlers on my wall would have impressed viewers, but I do not hunt to impress other people.

Like motherhood, that modern buzz phrase "quality of the hunt" sounds nice. But what is it supposed to mean in conjunction with management of the mule deer resource? Management only for the biggest possible heads? Nature already does that in some areas. One reason that Colorado produces a lopsidedly high proportion of trophy listings in Boone and Crockett is that it has more natural cover to protect bucks and allow them to live longer. In less naturally protected muley range, such management may increasingly demand manmade controls of the buck harvest.

Some hunters and writers say that we don't have to worry about overharvesting the big-buck gene pool (just as our forefathers were

How many of these mule-deer bucks have small racks because of immaturity and how many because of genetics? Author points out that very little is known about game management for genetics.

told not to worry about the unlimited supply of buffalo and passenger pigeons). The truth is that we know very little about that gene pool — except that such a resource can be overharvested as it was in Europe's red deer. European game managers learned the hard way generations ago to strictly control the harvest of prime superior-antlered stags. Overshoot them, and the whole gene pool of a given area's game is in trouble.

A dangerously simplistic alternative is the opposite step of legally reducing the kill of lesser-antlered bucks under the assumption they will then grow into big-antlered bucks. This can boomerang badly. It can mean the domination of a localized gene pool by poor-antler genetics. One commercial hunting ranch in Texas whitetail country almost ran out of trophy deer due to overshooting big-antlered bucks, thus surrendering the breeding to nontrophy bucks by default. Result — an increasing amount of inferior progeny.

Montana created a similar booby trap when the state forbade the harvest of spike bull elk in the Gravelly Mountains area. The objective was to let these supposedly juvenile spikes grow up to be big branch-antlered bulls. What game managers didn't realize is how many of the spikes were really fully mature, genetically inferior bulls incapable of growing decent racks, age notwithstanding. That was the natural result of too much previous "genetic skim" in overharvesting better-racked bulls.

Mistakenly protecting these small-antlered leftovers while still allowing the harvest of branch-antlered bulls meant the inferior permanent-spike bulls were saved to genetically sabotage their sons and grandsons, ad infinitum. (Maybe their daughters, too—one of the wild cards in game management is lack of data on the role of the genetics of female deer.)

Of course, the same thing can be done in mule deer genetics and perhaps already has occurred in heavily hunted areas—like eastern Wyoming—due simply to consistent overharvest of the best bucks. The Boone and Crockett records themselves strongly hint that those states producing very few book-trophy bucks have already suffered from genetic skimming in the past.

*   *   *

Game management has no magic wand to produce more super-racked bucks to meet growing demand. An obvious alternative is to stretch the limited supply of super bucks by restricting the individual hunter to one super buck every five years—or one per decade, *or* one per lifetime. Meaning that once a hunter has achieved his heart's desire of bagging a thirty-inch (or whatever) muley, he has to be content with lesser bucks in the future, since he's now had his theoretical share of a probably very limited supply of super bucks. This kind of "trophy management" would require mandatory postkill registration of *all* deer at legal checking stations (which some eastern states are doing as a sex harvest control).

Restrictive? Of course. Immorally or unfairly restrictive? Of course not! We *already have* similar restrictions that keep a hunter from even applying for any number of years for limited-lottery elk, mountain sheep, mountain goat, and moose permits if he has already drawn one. Similar restrictions on the harvest of super-buck muleys will outrage the obsessive headhunters, of course. But is the resource supposed to be managed for them or for other objectives, such as making sure that we continue to even *have* a resource of genetically high-quality bucks in the future? The argument that a hunter should be allowed to take all the super bucks he wants simply because he's capable of it has no merit. That's been the threadbare excuse for every blatant plundering of natural resources in our history.

To reduce hunting pressure, we already use lottery systems. Maybe we should try lotteries to stagger out when license holders can go hunting, so that all in a given state don't hit the hills simultaneously on opening day. Everyone agrees that "quality of the hunt" means not stumbling over too many competing hunters. But achieving this means we all get more control than in the past.

How long will we endure the Great Nonresident Rip-Off and Lock-Out? By what right does any state forbid nonresidents from hunting on federal lands which are *not* the exclusive property of that state or its citizens? Federal lands are the keystone of much western hunting, and those federal lands belong as much to Brooklyn as to Bozeman. We don't run Yellowstone Park campgrounds primarily for residents of Wyoming simply because the park is in Wyoming. Nor do we charge non-Wyoming folks fourteen times more admission fee to Yellowstone. Why should it be any different with other national recreational assets, including game living on national forests and BLM lands?

To prevent too much hunting pressure if national lands are open to all national citizens, the answer is simple. All license applications, resident and nonresident, should be lottery-drawn for federal lands in a given state. On nonfederal lands, of course, states should maintain full control of their wildlife resources. But federal lands should not be the private hunting preserve of state citizens as if they were the Norman nobility and the rest of us are conquered Saxon serfs with no rights on our own land.

American sportsmen, including mule deer hunters, had better prepare themselves to rationally discuss these and other tough questions in game-and-people management. Like it or not, American hunting will become more like that of Europe. It will become more tightly controlled or rationed because limited game resources cannot meet unlimited hunting-pressure demands. Again like Europe, hunting will become much costlier, since "added value" is the only way that game crops can compete against other revenue-producing land uses.

Population pressure alone is spelling an end to the come-all-ye free-and-easy sport hunting of the past. In my lifetime—and I'm only middle-aged, not ancient!—this country has gained an extra 100 million people. That's comparable to adding the entire population of Japan or twice the population of Great Britain. Meanwhile, none of the wildlife resource pies have gotten any bigger (some in fact have dwindled). But there are far more mouths per pie. Ergo, the slices must be smaller. And the number of second helpings, of necessity, must be limited. These aren't the only answers to our present and future wildlife management problems, but they may be part of the solution.

*   *   *

The mule deer resource's other people-management problems include the oil and coal stampede in the western states in the wake of the 1973 Arab oil boycott. Even though that great western energy boom fizzled in the mideighties, still there are unfavorable wildlife impacts from the regional population explosion caused by the boom.

Wildlife habitat losses to actual energy production infrastructure were largely insignificant. A developed oil field takes very little land out of potential mule deer use and, being largely automated, has negligible human disturbance. Even sizable strip mines take up extremely tiny tracts of land relative to the overall vastness of the West. The threat of scarce-water diversion to oil-shale processing is only a bad dream, since the most optimistic price projections for shale oil remain an impossible two to six times recent world oil prices. Another seventies energy boom seems unlikely in light of OPEC crumbling as a price-setting cartel. But we could see at least a smaller-screen replay of that scenario if either: 1) the U.S. puts a tax on foreign oil imports to protect our own oil industry and reduce our foreign trade deficit, or 2) Saudi oil supply is reduced by war or revolution.

Naturally, wildlife problems increased when energy boom areas like Campbell County, Wyoming (to name just one) quintupled in population. Along with multiplied legal hunting pressure came added poaching. The West is vast, the game wardens few. By and large, warden forces were not increased at the same rate as explosive population growth. A related factor is the universal advent of four-wheel-drive vehicles giving poachers tremendous mobility beyond reach of poorly equipped wildlife lawmen. As one Washington state wildlife agent plaintively told me, "My 4wd poachers are operating no-sweat back in country I can't get to in the 2wd street sedan the state issues me." It's high time that we demand more wildlife dollars for law enforcement. Many courts simply refuse to consider wildlife theft to be a basically criminal activity and let even repeat offenders off with the proverbial slap on the wrist. As cited, the great trophy hype of recent years has spawned a formidable renaissance of market hunting—big, easy dollars quickly inviting professionals.

Half-brothers to poachers are the too-numerous slob hunters. They result in many private lands being firmly closed to hunting. The fight against hunting slobbism starts with ourselves—how we hunt, how we conduct ourselves with landowners *and* other hunters, how we train our kids, right down to how we leave our campsites. One of life's unvarying rules is that people with self respect are never slobs. People with poor self images usually are.

*   *   *

An even worse result of the West's population boom is the loss of game habitat to people occupancy. Call it the suburbanization of the wide-open spaces, very often taking over limited winter range needed by big game. The late energy boom is only partly responsible for this. Much of it is due to our "loving the West to death," since many people find it an attractive place to live. This is particularly true of retirees, our fastest-growing population slice, many of whom "want a little place in the country" since cities are becoming scary places for seniors.

Much irreplaceable lowland winter range also has been lost to subdivision into vacation homes. Major ski developments can be serious offenders here, since they often include peripheral sprawls of cabins and condos. In all of this habitat invasion, human disturbance, free-running pet dogs, and snowmobiles are simply incompatible with much wildlife use, particularly in the high-stress winter period. Wildlife managers tell us that valley/lowland winter range availability is the biggest limiting factor in big-game populations, and those are exactly the areas being gobbled up in the West's latterday land rush.

Ironically, sportsmen are among the worst offenders here, since they are among the biggest buyers of such "ranchette" properties. A common sarcasm in many parts of the West is that a Doggoned Developer is some guy who wants to build himself a place up in the hills next year, while a True Conservationist is one who built *his* place up in the hills *last* year. In the comic strip immortality of "Pogo," we have met the enemy, and they is us.

*   *   *

The antihunters, like the poor, we have with us always. Although the more strident antihunting claque have wiped the foam off their mouths and quieted somewhat in recent years, don't be fooled. The antihunting movement hasn't gone away. It's just gone underground. Guess where. In some cases, right into our state and federal game agencies. Today an increasing amount of wildlife specialists are covert antihunters. How do I know that, you ask? Because I've been told that by experienced, reliable professionals in wildlife management whose judgment I trust.

New Wave wildlifers who resent hunting are as professionally out of place as traffic engineers who don't drive and further, dislike all who do. How then did this come about? It began with the big environmental uproar of the early 1970s. Many young Chicken Littles decided that the best way they could keep the sky from falling was to go into natural resources careers, which of course include wildlife work. These puerile Puritans, disliking hunting and hunters, are very anxious to set policies and regulations not to benefit wildlife but simply to shaft sport hunters. (Three centuries ago, they'd have burned witches.) But rarely will they admit it openly, for obvious reasons.

We sportsmen pay almost the entire wildlife-protection/management bill, including the salaries of professional wildlifers. In an age of budget cutbacks at all levels of government, it's amazing that antihunting wildlife professionals want to strangle their sole financial supporters. They expect resultant wildlife budget shortfalls to be made up from general tax revenues in lieu of hunting/fishing license fees and excise taxes on sporting goods.

They're dead wrong, of course. If these antihunting moles in wildlife management achieve their hearts' desire of regulatorily lynching sportsmen, they will simultaneously hang themselves with the other end of the same rope. Lacking enough revenue for such voter-sensitive priorities as public education and welfare, legislators and congressmen are not about to provide new wildlife money to replace what is no longer coming from sportsmen. When we have, for example, millions of low-income elderly living on cat food and garbage-can leftovers, don't kid yourself that lawmakers are going to blithely cough up wildlife payrolls to study the sex life of the great blue heron or how to mitigate mule deer winter loss.

In a few states, voters have authorized sales-tax add-ons to finance wildlife work. That is not the real answer. First, sales taxes are unpredictable revenue, subject to sharp drops due to recessions (as many states learned to their horror in the early 1980s). Second, getting more future money from fixed-rate taxes is like pulling teeth, all the more when you have to get the public to agree to it—a public that today does not look kindly on paying more taxes for any reason. By contrast, sportsmen are the only voluntary self-taxers in our history.

Meanwhile, how do sportsmen counter the antihunting movement among their hired hands in wildlife management? *Organize!* The historic weakness of sportsmen is their apathy. Strong, well-organized, broadly based sportsmen's groups have clout like you wouldn't believe. The National Rifle Association is an excellent example. While sportsmen are not going to change the emotional mindset of antihunters anywhere, we can make a political endrun around them to reach our lawmakers, governors, and game commissions.

Historically, the hunter is the American who has footed the entire bill for wildlife protection and enhancement through voluntary self-taxation (hunting-license fees and special excise taxes on sporting goods). Author says anti-hunters are wrong if they think general revenue taxes will pick up the slack if sport hunting's funding of wildlife ceases.

Take interest. Learn to ask why. Get the facts. Then fight for your rights by the usual democratic pressures of calls, letters, meetings, and petitions. In almost thirty years in newspaper and public relations work, I never cease to marvel at just how potent organized citizens can be when they get hot enough under the collar to heat the hindquarters of their public servants.

Years ago, the battle cry among sportsmen was to get politics out of conservation. Today, we should work hard to get the political process (it's called Democracy) back into conservation policy making. It's our only defense against the Trojan Horse of antihunting sentiment in professional wildlife bureaucracies — and the way to tackle some of the other resource problems, too.

*   *   *

Mule deer are great animals in a great land, and there are many of us who love them both. I sincerely believe that if we play our cards right, we will continue to behold and enjoy these big, gray deer. They are part of our heritage. From sun-seared hills, mule deer spotted the gleam of Spanish helmets in the mesquite, Lewis and Clark's men cordelling their flatboats up Big Muddy, and the packstrings of beaver plews wending down to the Green River rendezvous.

Muleys watched the dust-caked blue of the 7th jingling on to the Little Bighorn, the bawling longhorn herds coming up from Texas, and the first plow busting the virgin sod of the High Plains. Today they see traffic on our freeways and jet contrails in the Big Sky. Let's make sure that tomorrow there will still be mule deer — plenty of them in all their wide-racked glory — looking down at our children's children, too.

Bibliography

Back, Joe. *Horses, Hitches, and Rocky Trails.* Boulder, CO: Johnson Books, Inc., 1979.

Colin, Fraser. *The Avalanche Enigma.* Chicago: Rand McNally and Company.

Dalrymple, Byron W. *The Complete Book of Deer Hunting.* Tulsa, OK: Winchester Press, 1973.

Dalrymple, Byron W. *Deer Hunting with Dalrymple: A Lifetime of Lore on the Whitetail & Mule Deer.* New York: Arco Publishing, Inc., 1983.

Darner, Kirt I. *How to Find Giant Bucks.* Marceline, MO: Walsworth Publishing Company, Inc., 1984.

Dasmann, William. *If Deer Are to Survive.* Harrisburg, PA: Stackpole Books, Inc., 1971.

DeFalco, Joe. *Field Dressing, Skinning, Butchering, and Cooking Deer.*

Elman, Robert, and George Peper. *Hunting America's Game Animals & Birds.* Tulsa, OK: Winchester Press, 1980.

Knap, Jerome J. *The Complete Outdoorsman's Handbook.* Toronto, Ont.: Pagurian Press, Ltd., 1974.

Meteorology for Naval Aviators. Office of The Chief of Naval Operations.

NRA Firearms & Ammunition Fact Book. National Rifle Association.

O'Connor, Jack. *The Rifle Book.* Westminster, MD: Alfred A. Knopf, Inc., 1978.

Ormond, Clyde. *Outdoorsman's Handbook*. New York: Berkeley Publishing Corp., 1975.

Outdoor Life Deer Hunter's Yearbook. New York: Outdoor Life Books, annual editions.

Prater, Gene. *Snowshoeing*. Seattle, WA: Mountaineers Books, 1980.

Riviere, Bill. *Backcountry Camping*. Garden City, NY: Dolphin Books, 1972.

Rue, Leonard Lee. *The Deer of North America*. New York: Crown Publishing, Inc., 1979.

Sell, Francis E. *The Art of Successful Deer Hunting*. Oshkosh, WI: Willow Creek, 1980.

Seton, Ernest Thompson. *Lives of Game Animals*. New York: Doubleday, 1929.

Stebbins, Ray. *Cold-Weather Camping*. Chicago: Contemporary Books, Inc., 1979.

Wallmo, Olof C., ed. *Mule and Black-tailed Deer of North America*. Lincoln, NE: University of Nebraska Press, 1981.

Zumbo, Jim, and Robert Elman, eds. *All-American Deer Hunter's Guide*. Piscataway, NJ: New Century Publishers, Inc., 1984

Zumbo, Jim. *Hunting America's Mule Deer*. Tulsa, OK: Winchester Press, 1981.

Index

Some other fine hunting books
from America's Great Outdoor Publisher

Bird Hunting with Dalrymple
The rewards of shotgunning across North America.
by Byron W. Dalrymple

Art and Science of Whitetail Hunting
How to interpret the facts and find the deer.
by Kent Horner

Hunting Rabbits and Hares
The complete guide to North America's favorite small game.
by Richard P. Smith

White-tailed Deer: Ecology & Management
Developed by the Wildlife Management Institute. Over 2,400 references on
every aspect of deer behavior.
edited by Lowell K. Halls

Quail Hunting in America
Tactics for finding and taking quail by season and habitat.
by Tom Huggler

Bowhunting for Whitetails
Your best methods for taking North America's favorite deer.
by Dave Bowring

Deer & Deer Hunting
The serious hunter's guide.
by Dr. Rob Wegner

Elk of North America
The definitive, exhaustive, classic work on the North American elk.
ed. by Jack Ward Thomas and Dale E. Toweill

Pronghorn, North America's Unique Antelope
The practical guide for hunters.
by Charles L. Cadieux

Spring Turkey Hunting
The serious hunter's guide.
by John M. McDaniel

How to Plan Your Western Big Game Hunt
All you need to know to plan a do-it-yourself or guided hunt in the 11
Western states.
by Jim Zumbo

**Available at your local bookstore, or for complete ordering information,
write:**

Stackpole Books
Dept. MD
Cameron and Kelker Streets
Harrisburg, PA 17105

**For fast service credit card users may call 1-800-READ-NOW
In Pennsylvania, call 717-234-5041**